Nontraditional

Nontraditional
Life Lessons from a Community College

by Nan Kuhlman

AnnorlundaBooks

To my husband Craig who has made my life an adventure

Contents

Prologue

The topic of our class discussion was "deadbeat dads," spurred by the reading of John Cheever's "Reunion," a short essay about a boy's disappointment with his estranged father.[1] The students in my class jumped at the chance to point out the father's missteps: his drinking, his belligerent treatment of those he considers beneath his social status, his obvious "showing off" to impress his son. I asked them to talk about examples that Cheever uses to illustrate, and in the course of the discussion, one student said, "That was my dad. He acted just like that." Others concurred that they experienced similar "deadbeat dads," and how they hoped for a better relationship but never saw it happen.

Then one older student, a graying former Marine, said, "Well, I see this story differently. I see a father who desperately wants to connect with his son, but who's probably nervous. This son may not have seen his father

---

[1] Cheever, John. "Reunion." *The Millennium Reader*, edited by Stuart Hirschberg and Terry Hirschberg, Pearson Education, Inc., 2009, pp. 151-154.

for three years, but the story doesn't tell us if the mother kept the child away from him. I see the son judging the father and creating the division, and the father is trying to win him back."

At that moment, the class shifted; the perspective had been enlarged. We realized intuitively that this former Marine had been in the father's shoes, and I asked the class, "Why did most of us side with the son in our discussion? What technique does Cheever use to make most of us feel that way?" The students nodded in agreement, murmuring "The first-person point of view" and seeing with new eyes how an author's use of a literary technique can sway readers. More importantly, the class recognized its own bias, the crazy way our minds tell us how the world is. It was moments like this one that made me slog through stacks of grading because I got to witness this expansion as students broke free of negative thought patterns and traditional mindsets into a nontraditional way of thinking.

The term "nontraditional" is often used in academia to describe students who are not the typical college student, a recent high school graduate with college prep experience. Community colleges like the one where I teach typically have an open enrollment policy that welcomes all who wish to learn. Our college has veterans who are taking advantage of the GI bill now their tour of duty is completed; some of them, like Jared, are wrestling with the demons from PTSD. Many of our students qualify for Pell Grants and other types of financial aid, despite the fact that the tuition is only around $3500 a year for fall and spring semesters. A number of them, like Norma, struggle to feed and house their families. Often they are working one or two part-time jobs along with raising children. Sometimes they are dislocated factory workers, like Margie and Shari, hoping to retrain for another job. The age of the students ranges from younger than fifteen (high school students taking college courses for dual credits) to nearly sixty. This student body is nontraditional in the fullest sense of the word, and so is at least one of the instructors.

Nontraditional also described my entrance into academic work. Homeschooling our three children was my first priority, my freelance magazine writing for a couple of local magazines was my second, and far off in the future was the dream of a master's degree and teaching at a college. One evening I was attending a business presentation for my husband's firm (a spousal obligation), listening to an economist make predictions about the stock market and wondering if the caterer would be serving those delicious stuffed mushrooms and bacon-wrapped water chestnuts. As we mixed and mingled with business clients, enjoying hors d'oeuvres after the presentation, my husband introduced me to the president of a rural community college nearby. "We're always looking for adjunct instructors, especially for composition," he told me.

"But I don't have a master's degree," I stammered.

He reassured me, "We have ways around that for people who have work experience. Why don't you email your resumé to the dean of Arts and Sciences and tell her you spoke with me?"

The students come to the college, just like I did, looking for second chances, somewhat wounded and in need of healing. These stories are true, though the names have been changed and some of the details are combined to provide anonymity. We are all nontraditional, and we're hoping that this place of higher learning might teach us how to think outside the boundaries that we place on ourselves and others.

Chapter 1
Who Do You Think You Are?

Fortunetellers and Futures

Like any other eighteen-year-old, I wasn't sure what I wanted to be when I grew up. I toyed with the idea of the theater, having enjoyed my high school plays and musicals, and I suggested to my parents that I could go to New York in the company of a somewhat effeminate male classmate who was also interested in theater to give off-Broadway a try. That was shot down faster than the skeet my cousins used for target practice in the field behind our house. "You need to be able to get a real job," my mother counseled as she lassoed my youthful optimism and brought it back to northwestern Ohio earth.

I looked through college majors and landed on this one: Radio, TV, Film. It sounded like it would be interesting, and it might allow me to work in front of a camera, which pleased my youthful narcissism. My parents approved reluctantly, and I set off to learn about the world of the media, which even in the 1980s was changing wildly.

My first media class was a standard overview of the way television stations worked, outlining all the sleep-inducing regulations by the Federal Communications Commission. But the professor said something interesting, something that my girlfriends and I could not fathom: that the newly developed cable TV would provide endless channels of programming and that programming would be very specific to a particular demographic. We had grown up with three channels (four if you counted PBS) that represented the three major networks: CBS, NBC, and ABC. My professor told us about the potential of cable and how this would allow advertisers to target their audience better and how it would give the audience more viewing options. He prophesied about having hundreds of channels, and our eyes almost rolled back in our heads, just contemplating all the content we would have to choose from. This would be too good to be true. Our viewing options wouldn't be restricted to *General Hospital* or *Dynasty*; we would be empowered with choices. This would be particularly important if the university wasn't running its Free Friday Movie Night or if there weren't other campus activities going on.

For those of us not involved in Greek life, campus activities put on by the student body organization helped alleviate the boredom that often accompanied a keg of "low" beer and hints of a party. Our dorm hosted a Halloween party like this, and I had rented a costume from the campus theater. It was a tavern wench costume, or as I called it, "a sexy peasant dress," with a deeply-scooped neckline, tightly-fitted bodice, puffy sleeves, and long full skirt. Though I lacked the bosom to fill it out to its best capacity, my roommate still said I looked "scrumptious."

We made our way down to the dorm common space, a large room with great windows and a piano that had an A ♭ in the lower treble octave that tended to stick when played. No one was making music on the piano now; instead, Freddie Mercury was singing about biting the dust and AC/DC was on a personal highway to hell. My roommate, clad in her father's Army dress uniform from the Korean War, led the charge as we snaked our way through the mass of gyrating bodies, finally landing in a secure spot on the fringes. As we sang along with Blondie's "Call Me," I felt a tap on my shoulder, and I turned around to face a girl named Sarah who lived on my floor. Her eyes were red and mascara-streaked her cheeks. She spat out the slurred words, "Stay away from him, or so help me God, I'll beat you to a pulp."

The music blared, and while I knew something was wrong, I wasn't sure I heard her correctly. "What? What's wrong?" I yelled back as helpfully as I could.

"You heard me," she said as she took a step forward, menacingly. "You got no business talking to him."

I stepped back and stared at her, unsure what she was talking about. I knew she had a boyfriend because I had seen him around, but I had never met him. Before I could respond, her roommate grabbed her, saying, "That's not her. She's over here." Without any further explanation, they moved through the crowd toward the perpetrator of this alleged flirtation.

"Well, you asked for it. That's what happens when you look like a tavern wench," my roommate said, laughing. "What a lightweight! I can't believe Sarah's drunk already."

It was true: one could get just as drunk on low beer as high beer. It simply took a larger quantity, and Sarah had obviously been working on it for a while before the party started. Once we danced and sang and had our fill of watery low beer, we decided to see what else the campus had planned to celebrate Halloween.

The student body organization had created a haunted student union (who would have thought?), and my roommate and I decided to go through it. Fake spider webs and eerie lighting transformed what were standard, innocuous meeting rooms in the union building to horror chambers where ghoulish costumed figures would moan and lurch, grasping for warm human flesh. Once we made it through the haunted union exhibit intact, we noticed a sign that said, "Tarot Cards and Auras Read: $1.00." The price was right, and I sat down to have my cards read, something I had never done before. The fortuneteller, wearing the typical garb with gold hoop earrings I could put my fist through, placed three cards on the table. "I see a man in a suit in your future," she said in a low voice that exuded confidence. "Are you involved in any legal issues right now?"

I laughed, "No, fortunately not," my skepticism over the accuracy of tarot card readers affirmed. The other two cards seemed equally off-base. I thanked her and got up to leave when in a desperate effort to restore her credibility she said, "Wait—let me read your aura. You have a strong yellow aura. Are you an education major? Are you going to be a teacher?"

"No," I said smiling, shaking my head. "I'm in Radio, TV, and Film. Thanks anyway."

Exploring the Bandwidth

He reminded me of an elf, a good elf that one might picture in a modern fairy tale. Logan sat in the front row from the very first day of class, giving me a close-up look at the tattoos on each arm and his asymmetrical haircut. Choosing to be close enough to see spit fly was an unusual occurrence for most of my students, so he seemed ready to learn.

The first writing assignment was to write a narrative about an event or a person that changed the student's view of the world. Many of the narratives I read dealt with loss and what was gained by losing: an appreciation of the present after the loss of a loved one, the joy of caring for another after the loss of freedom from having a child, or the profound awareness of taking charge of one's life following the loss of a relationship. Logan's essay talked about the loss of a relationship. After high school graduation, his girlfriend went off to Ohio University in southern Ohio, and he was left at home, unsure of the next step.

He saw his path involving music, sharing that he was self-taught on a number of instruments and part of a local grunge band. They landed a manager who had some connections, and their manager secured six months of engagements in five or six states. His narrative described how the manager sought to create a particular image for the band, advising the members not to wash their hair for a few days to create a greasy, piecey look. Wearing black and having tattoos was imperative. His job at the local pet supply store allowed him six months of leave, so he went on tour, hoping to forget the girlfriend and strike it big with his band.

He enjoyed some of the aspects of the tour: the music, the novelty of new venues, and the attention of fans. But the road can be difficult, and for a start-up band, this is particularly true. "Sometimes we had to sleep in the van if we didn't make enough money at a show," Logan shared with me when I asked about the tour. "Five guys with our equipment, all in a minivan," he shook his head in disbelief even though he had done it. "I remember sleeping, sitting up, with my guitar in my lap and my feet on a keyboard case."

Even when a hotel room was provided, it was the cheapest (and maybe not the cleanest) one they could find. This may have deterred some, but for Logan, it was the lack of time he had to work on his music that bothered him, and he yearned to take time to create. By the end of the six months, he knew he had to return home to work at the pet supply store and go to school.

His ACT scores and high school GPA were not enough on their own to get him into Ohio University, though now the girlfriend was just a friend and his motivation was the music-recording major the institution offered. Logan came to our community college with the hopes of creating a good GPA while fulfilling some general education requirements at a much lower tuition rate.

This was where I met him, in the front row of an eight-week accelerated writing class. He was an engaged student, quick to contribute, nodding his head when a point made sense to him. After class one day, I told him how pleased I was with the work he was submitting. "This class is really different from the first time I took it," he confessed.

"How's that?" I asked.

"I don't know. I could say it was the instructor last time, but I think I just needed to grow up some," he replied with a thoughtful look on his face. "And after living on the road, it was hard to make myself do something that I was afraid of."

"So writing scares you?"

He nodded, the asymmetrical chunk of hair flopping forward. "I'm afraid that I'll sound stupid."

"Everyone feels like that at first," I told him as we walked together toward the door. "It's like shooting basketball free throws. If you only shoot once a month, you're probably not going to be very good. But if you shoot some every day, you'll really see some progress."

"You think so?" he questioned, stopping in his tracks to look at me. "I sure hope you're right."

Standardized testing, like the ACT and SAT, were thorns in Logan's side, so he decided to take this topic on for his research project. After a weekend of research, Logan came to class, excited to share what he'd learned. "Mrs. Kuhlman, did you know that not only are tests like the ACT and SAT biased against minorities and kids who don't speak English as their first language, but they're also biased against women?" He pulled a stack of copies from his book bag, flipping through until he found the article. "Here it says that women score as much as sixty points lower than men on both the verbal and math parts of the SAT. And minority women score even lower than that."[2]

---

[2] Connor, Katherine, and Ellen J. Vargyas. "The Legal Implications of Gender Bias in Standardized Testing." *The Berkeley Journal of Gender, Law & Justice*, vol. 7, no. 1, 2013, pp. 13-89. *Berkley Law*, scholarship.law.berkeley.edu/cgi/viewcontent.cgi?article=1063&contex t=bglj.

His comments about gender bias caught the attention of several female classmates, who hovered around discussing their own ACT woes. Logan shared what he had learned, encouraging them to stop beating themselves up for less-than-stellar scores when the fairness of standardized testing was being hotly debated.

As the accelerated term moved quickly, Logan began to develop the discipline needed to meet all the assignment deadlines, something he didn't do with the first composition course. He had no more time to waste, and the vision of a career in music recording spurred him on. After the first composition course, he tagged along with me for advanced composition, another general education requirement. Later I received an email from him with good news: he had been accepted into Ohio University's music recording and production program.

"You know," he said to me after our last class, "I wasn't sure I could tackle school again after I bombed the first semester. I never really liked writing until these classes, but now writing papers doesn't faze me. I think if this music thing doesn't fly, I could be a writer."

Sticking His Neck Out

"You know, Mrs. Kuhlman," Barry told me one day. "I've even started watching my grammar in my text messages to my kids." Barry was a divorced dad of three kids, ages eight, eleven, and fourteen.

"You're kidding, Barry," I said. "I don't do that. I'll use "i" or "u" freely in text speak."

"I guess I hear you in my head. 'Don't use the pronoun you, Barry. Reread what you've written, Barry,'" he joked as he loaded his backpack with books after our writing workshop. "I just can't seem to shut you off."

"Well, I'm giving you permission right now to use a "u" for the pronoun you in a text, just not in our academic papers, OK?" I teased back. "So what topic are you thinking about for your research paper?"

Barry sat the heavy backpack down on a desk. "I can't make up my mind. I thought about doing the legalization of marijuana in the state of Ohio, but I'm not sure that would be a good paper to have in my digital writing portfolio, especially with my history."

"I've had lots of students write about the legalization of marijuana, and some of them were good and some were not-so-good. Why don't you think that would be a good topic for you?" I asked, curious about his sudden reserve.

He ran a hand through his hipster-undercut hair and looked around to see if we were alone in the classroom. "I'm a convicted felon," he said, shaking his head. "It started with drug charges when I was a juvenile. I spent some time in juvenile detention, and I really only went to high school through tenth grade. When I got out and turned eighteen, I was caught again and spent a couple years in jail. That's where I got my GED. It's funny. Every intelligence test I took when I was in jail showed that I was above average in intelligence. They'd say to me, 'Barry, you got no business being in here. You're smarter than that.' I had a lot of growin' up to do." He smiled when he said it, like he finally understood, maybe even forgave himself a little. "After I got out, I landed this factory job, but every six months I got laid off. This time, though, I decided I was going to make a change."

"That's got to be exciting—changing your future," I said. "You've been making progress. I've seen it—haven't you? I mean, if you're starting to correct your text messages..."

Barry laughed. "Yeah, I guess I have seen some progress. But I still don't know what I should write about for this big paper."

"Tell me what you're interested in," I encouraged him.

"Sports—I like sports. When I was in high school, before I went to juvie, I played every sport: football, basketball, baseball. I loved them all. I was pretty good, too." His face became sober. "That all went away when I was in jail. I still enjoy going to my son's ball games, though, and I play on some intramural softball teams in the summer."

"I'm glad to hear that you're still able to play since you enjoyed it so much. Have you thought about arguing about a salary cap for baseball players? I've had some students write about that topic, and there seemed to be plenty of sources."

Barry looked interested. "Yeah, that's something that I've read a little about, and I think I could do that." His demeanor perked up a little, and he waved a paper at my face, grinning. "Since you helped with that problem, maybe you can help with this electrical engineering problem."

I put up my two first fingers in the sign of a cross as if his math-related engineering problem was a vampire going for my carotid artery. "Not my expertise. Is that your major? How did you decide on that?"

Barry propped his foot on a chair. "When I got laid off from the factory and had this chance to go to school for free through that Ohio Means Jobs program, I knew this was my last chance to get a decent job, one where I didn't have to worry so much about layoffs and where I could finally get past having that felony on my record. So I looked at what the college offered, and when I saw electrical engineering, I thought, *that looks interesting. I think I'd like to learn about that.*"

"That's all it took? And you didn't have any previous knowledge of electrical circuits and the like?" I asked, thinking that his choice of careers sounded much like reaching into a grab bag of career choices blindfolded.

"Well, I was always pretty good at math, at least from what I remember from tenth grade. Since I lost the last two years of high school, I feel like I really missed a lot, especially with this writing. But math is coming back to me pretty quickly." He slipped the backpack over his shoulders. "Well, I think I'll start researching salary caps for baseball players. Thanks for talking me through that."

Barry's writing mimicked the way he talked. On his rough drafts, I would have to mark out all the "wells" and clichéd phrases that filled his papers. "Your writing is too conversational," I would tell him. "If you were writing for a blog, it would be great because it feels just like someone talking to the reader. But with academic writing, you have to learn to write more formally. You want to sound super-smart, not like you're talking to your buddy." I encouraged him to take his rough drafts to the Writing Lab for proofreading to help him weed out the "you" pronouns, "wells," and clichés. He brought back a draft from the Writing Lab that had so many corrections, it seemed overwhelming, even to me.

Barry just laughed. "Look what she did, that Writing Lab tutor. She pencil-whipped the shit out of my draft."

"That she did," I laughed, agreeing with him. "Let me look through her marks and we'll see if they all need to be done." My experience with other students' drafts that came back from the Writing Lab showed me that there was a great variance between faculty tutors when it came to the issue of commas. In one instance, a particular faculty tutor inserted over twenty commas in what I thought was already a well-written student draft. Barry's paper, however, had a number of wording errors, and the "pencil-whipping" his draft received was well-deserved.

As the semester progressed, Barry's writing improved though he still had to rely on "pencil-whipping" from the Writing Lab to make his essays the best they could be. More importantly, his attitude about writing changed. After our last class together, when all the other students had gone, Barry came up to my desk. "Mrs. Kuhlman, I know you write articles for magazines and such, and I was wondering if you had any ideas where I might send a children's book that I've written."

"Wow! A children's book? Tell me the summary of the story."

"It's about a little giraffe that screws up and needs a second chance to show the others that he can be a leader," Barry said quietly as if he were concerned that someone might overhear and steal his original idea.

"Sounds interesting. Did you illustrate it, too?"

Barry's face broke into a wide smile. "Yeah, I did. It was a lot of fun to work on, despite being busy with my classes. I've always liked to dabble with art, and my daughter had these markers, all sorts of colors, and I went crazy drawing giraffes."

We talked a little more about writing, publishing, and self-publishing, and after he left, I put his reflective essay, his last assignment, in my bag. In the corner, he had written a note: "Thanks for being my teacher." Beside it was a tiny giraffe.

Breaking Up, Breaking Through, and Breaking Free

Her timidity almost had a form of its own, the way she held herself closely as if she were cold or afraid or both. June's appearance also revealed a subliminal wish to be invisible, her clothing shapeless for a twenty-year-old, her hair clean but unstyled. Though she sat in the front row of my advanced composition class, her voice was little more than a whisper when I called on her to answer a question.

One day our discussion was about the life and writing of Helen Keller, a woman who lived from the late 1800s to mid-1900s. She became both blind and deaf following an illness as a toddler yet managed to graduate from college, becoming a celebrated writer and speaker.[3] When I was growing up, Helen Keller was an example touted by my schoolteachers, encouraging us to learn from her grit and tenacity. "So who can describe Helen Keller's breakthrough moment?" I asked the class.

"It was at the well," a student named Roy offered. "Her teacher Anne Sullivan spelled the sign language for the word 'water' in her hand as she held it under the pump."

Another student added, "Yeah, she acted like an animal before that, taking food from others' plates, breaking things."

---

[3] Keller, Helen. "The Day Language Came into My Life." *The Millennium Reader*, edited by Stuart Hirschberg and Terry Hirschberg, Pearson Education, Inc., 2009, pp. 229-231.

"What did she compare her life to before she understood language?" I asked. "What was the metaphor she used?" Out of the corner of my eye, I saw June's hand creep up. "Yes, June?"

"She said she felt like she was a ship in a fog, and she needed help to find her way," June said, her voice low but certain. "When she learned that everything had a name, her world began to have meaning." She sat back in her chair, and I knew that she had offered her one and only contribution to the class discussion for that day.

After she missed class a couple of times, I followed up by email to see what was going on. June emailed back, saying, "I'm sorry I've missed class. I take care of my grandparents who have dementia, plus I work part-time at the market in town. On top of that, my car has been acting up, I didn't have a ride to class, and our internet was out. I'll be there next week, and I'll have the writing exercises done." Her email picture showed her smiling face posed with arms around a horse's neck, a stark contrast to the face I saw June wear in the classroom.

True to her word, June was in class the next meeting, and I pulled her aside afterward to see how she was doing on her larger project. Eyes downcast, June said, "I'm sorry, Mrs. Kuhlman. I've been out of it lately. Family troubles." Her brows furrowed. "Guy troubles."

"Are your grandparents not well?" I asked her.

"They're as well as they're going to be. They both have some dementia. The main reason I live with them is because my dad is a colossal jerk who says I never do anything right, that I'm stupid and I'll never make it through school. My mom doesn't say anything, just lets him talk to me that way. I guess I shouldn't be surprised; he talks to her that way, too," she said, and I noticed her shoulders rounding even more than usual as if those words were a heavy weight upon her. "I'm showing them that I can be independent, that I can hold a job, take care of Grandma and Grandpa, and get through school, too. Sometimes it seems like I have to fight my way forward, though."

"It sounds like you have a lot going on. I'm just a little concerned that you're going to get behind on this bigger project. Tell me about your topic, and I'll see if I can help you find sources."

June perked up as she described her topic: making it legal to own a wolf or a hybrid wolfdog as a pet and requiring veterinarians to administer the rabies vaccine to them. Animals were a soft spot for June, that much was clear, and after she spelled out her topic, we took a minute to look together on the library database for sources. Within a few minutes, June had sent links to her student email for five or six promising sources. "Thanks for the help, Mrs. Kuhlman," she said. "I should be able to work on this project more over the next few days. Oh, I almost forgot." She reached into her bag and pulled out a couple of tattered writing exercises. "Here are the writing exercises I owe you." She walked out of the room, books tightly clasped to her chest, her bag slung on one rounded shoulder.

One of the exercises June had completed was a response to this prompt: Describe a time where you had a "breakthrough" similar to what Helen Keller experienced. June's response went something like this:

> I had a breakthrough somewhat like Helen Keller's recently, but my breakthrough didn't have the same type of happy ending. I trusted a guy who said he loved me and that he thought I was beautiful. I did everything he wanted just to make him happy, so why wasn't that enough? My breakthrough happened when he broke up with me for another girl. I understand now that I can't trust men to be kind or truthful with me. It's probably just me because I'm not that smart or pretty, but after dealing with my dad and my ex, I have learned that guys can be cruel. I'm tired of people being mean to me.

Her pain came through these few words on a page, and I blinked away tears as I put the wrinkled page on the desk. Her situation reminded me of our chickens that we had on the farm where I grew up. If one of them became a little weak or sick, the others would peck at it until it died from its injuries unless we noticed and rescued it in time. Even once we put the injured chicken in a solitary pen, sometimes it still didn't make it. It almost seemed like it gave up despite our efforts to nurse it back to health.

"June, this guy was a jerk, but not all guys are. It's not your fault," I wrote on her exercise. My words seemed inadequate and lame, but I wanted to put some salve on those wounds pecked into her heart. Helen Keller called her breakthrough "the light of love,"[4] but some breakthroughs leave us unsure of who we are and what we might offer the world.

Love Trumps Career

I majored in Radio, TV, and Film until I realized that a career in this meant I would be behind the camera or in the control room of a studio. At eighteen, I wanted to be in front of the camera, so I changed my major to journalism, and, not content with simply being a name on a page, I majored in broadcast journalism. My advisor compared me to a well-known local TV anchor, another alumnus of our university, saying, "You could be the next one." That's probably what they paid advisors to do, boost the egos of their graduates, though mine was fairly inflated all by itself.

---

[4] Ibid, 230.

I was news director of one of the campus radio stations, and this gave me an entry into an internship at the local radio stations in Findlay, doing news on the weekend. Though I enjoyed working with news, covering local campaigns and community issues, I knew my prospects were going to be limited because I no longer wanted to move far from Ohio. I was in love.

During my senior year, I tried to take steps to gain some experience and training beyond broadcast journalism. I took a few public relations writing courses, and I picked up a brief internship working for the PR division of the university. I graduated with the top GPA in the school of journalism, only to spend the next ten months unemployed.

Each day I looked through the classified ads for jobs in our small community. There weren't many, and most of them wouldn't even let me interview. They said I was overqualified for a typical office job, fearing that once they trained me, I'd leave for a journalism job. Clearly, they had no clue that with only one newspaper in our town of about twenty thousand people, two radio stations, and no television stations, my chances for employment in my field of study were slim. If I was only concerned about landing a job in my field of study, I would have moved to a bigger city, a different state. By this time, though, I was thinking about a wedding, and I could not, would not, did not want to leave our small town. Love took priority over work.

One snowy day in late February, I received a call back from a local insurance agency asking if I could come in for an interview. The snowfall was expected to become heavier, dropping up to six inches, which would make traveling on country roads a little hazardous. I told the owner, "I can make it," and then I called my dad for reassurance. "You can make it into town," he said, "and I'll follow you home."

I put on my interviewing suit, olive green with a cream-colored bow blouse and brown pumps. I bought it anticipating lots of interviews, but other than wearing it to church, it had scarcely been broken in. The snow covered the tips of my patent leather pumps as I shuffled out to the barn to the silver Ford Pinto, the very one I wanted to buy from my dad if I got this job, any job. The roads weren't bad as I traveled from the rural countryside into the city limits, but the snowfall had picked up, giant flakes flying fast and furious and beginning to mound on the sidewalks and lawns.

The owner, Harry Murphy, greeted me at the door, face friendly and florid. "Thanks for coming in today." As we walked to his office, we chitchatted about the weather, and he cracked the first of many jokes: "One way to beat out the competition is to show up for the job interview when no one else wants to come out in the snow. Was that your plan?"

I laughed and nodded. "Absolutely."

He sat down behind a large wooden desk that seemed to take up most of the office and motioned for me to take a seat across from him. "So...I see you have a journalism degree?"

"Yes." I knew this question would come up, and I had rehearsed my answer. "At the time I started the journalism major, I had no boyfriend and no prospects of marriage. Here I am now, graduated with a journalism degree, but now I have a boyfriend. As soon as he graduates, we're getting married. He already works for First National Bank, so we want to stay in Findlay."

Harry smiled knowingly. "The newspaper and radio stations aren't hiring, huh?"

I shook my head. "I'm not even sure I want to be a journalist anymore. When I started this major, I had no plans to be married and have a family. I was going to move away from here. Now I see that with journalism's crazy hours...well, it probably won't work. I need a job with set hours I can count on." The long months of unemployment spurred me on, and I plunged ahead, almost desperately. "I can do a good job for you if you give me a chance."

"Let's talk some more, and I have a math test I'd like you to take. It's not timed, so there's no pressure." He grinned. "At least there's not that much pressure."

He explained about the insurance clerk position and how I would need to become an agent for ease in assisting customers. This would mean taking a two-day class in Columbus to prepare for the test, with the licensing test the next day. "I don't have any problems taking tests," I told him confidently. "You can see from my GPA that I did well in school."

He skimmed my brief resumé thoughtfully. "So you want to leave journalism behind and start something new?"

"Yes, I do," I said with more confidence than I felt, feeling as if I were giving up my firstborn child but wanting to move forward with something, anything.

That day I received the highest score the owner of the insurance agency had ever seen from an applicant on the simple math test he required, and I got the job. Not a journalism job, but a job. With benefits. A new start, and not all new starts come with benefits.

Chapter 2
The Difficulties of New Starts

Getting Lost and Finding Dreams

There were two administrative assistants in Harry's small insurance agency: Myrna sat at the second desk and I sat at the first, closest to the front door. I was the front line, greeting customers, helping with their concerns, or directing them to the appropriate salesman's office. Though I knew how to figure insurance quotes and complete applications for home and personal auto insurance, I couldn't sign the application because I was not yet a licensed agent in the state of Ohio. Still, there was plenty to keep me busy, including collecting rent from Harry's upstairs tenants.

Harry had two residential apartments above the office, and they were rented to two brothers and an elderly lady named Margaret. One of the brothers was a cook at a nearby restaurant, and the other brother, Bob, was a self-employed handyman. Once a month, Bob would bring their rent to the office, all in cash, and then he would engage in what might be called flirting with Myrna and me.

Harry was always quick to tease us about it. "You know, I've seen Bob naked," Harry began. "One night I had to come up to the office late to pick up some papers for an early morning meeting. I had to park across the street, and as I looked up, I saw Bob standing in front of the window, completely naked. I'm not sure if he was advertising or if he just woke up."

Bob would stride purposefully in, with hands in his jeans pockets and a cap cocked on the back of his head, then casually toss the wad of bills on the counter. "So-uh, what's up with yous girls?" he'd ask Myrna and me. Myrna's experience with Bob's routine made her more patient with him than I was, and she'd respond, "Well, Bob, we're just doin' our best to sell insurance. You need any today?"

"Aww, yous girls know I come down here just to see some pretty faces, not to buy insurance," he'd say. "Hell, if Harry had his way, I'd be up to my ears in insurance."

As she wrote out his receipt, Bob would regale us with his tales of his experiences with customers, usually involving some of his physical prowess, and then he would end the conversation, "Well, yous girls have a good one." As he left, Myrna and I would look at each other and shake our heads, unable to forget Harry's story about Bob's late night window-flashing.

I was scheduled to travel to Columbus in April for a review class, stay overnight, and then take the agent's licensing test the next morning. Harry was paying for the whole process, including my mileage for the two-hour trip to Columbus and back. "Just keep your receipts for food and keep track of your mileage," he told me before I left.

The next morning at 5:30 a.m. I took off for the west side of Columbus in the dark and the rain. It was long before the days of GPS and Google Maps, so I was relying on directions I had written down after consulting a map. As I neared Columbus, traffic became more congested and I was pinned between two semis, making it near impossible to see road signs. As I approached the I-270 outer belt that circled Columbus, I knew I needed to go right. Straining to see past wipers flipping back and forth at top speed, I caught a glimpse of the sign that said "I-270." I had no time to read more than that as the entrance ramp to the right appeared, so I followed the first semi on to the outer belt.

The entrance ramp soon curved around, looping me to travel east, but being directionally challenged, I didn't realize it. After traveling for twenty or thirty minutes, I knew something was wrong, but to backtrack would make me later than if I just continued looping around Columbus. Though I had allowed plenty of time to make it there, I ended up being a few minutes late to my review class because of the "detour."

The class was a review of insurance terms with a lot of "when you see this phrase, you choose this answer." That made taking the insurance agent licensing exam a breeze the next day, and I returned to the office in Findlay that afternoon to submit my receipts and mileage. Traveling home in the daylight *sans* rain made a difference and I easily navigated my way back to Findlay.

Harry took my receipts, and before he could look at my mileage, I offered an embarrassed explanation: "You don't have to pay me all the mileage I have there. I ended up getting on I-270 East instead of West, and I went all the way around Columbus." My face felt hot, but Harry laughed.

"That's OK. You were lost on my time," he said as he wrote out the check to reimburse me.

After our May wedding, my husband had to make the same trek toward Columbus in the fall to take a review class for the licensing test to trade securities. As it turned out, he was the only student in the review class, so his instructor spent a lot of time talking about life and life choices.

"If you could do anything," the instructor asked, "what would you do?"

My husband Craig's response was immediate: "Go to our church's college for a theology degree and be a pastor."

"Then that's what you should do," the instructor encouraged. "You're young, you don't have kids—what's stopping you?"

Before he returned home, Craig had completed and mailed the application to go to our denomination's college for a bachelor's in theology. "You're not going to like this, but hear me out," he began. He gave all the reasons he wanted to go, saying, "I don't know if I'll even be accepted, but I had to try."

I tearfully knew it was the right decision for him, and I hoped that applying would get the notion of moving to California out of his system. "How am I supposed to find my way around Los Angeles?" I snapped, grasping for ways that his plan wouldn't work. "I get lost just trying to go to Columbus!"

He put his arms around me and whispered in my ear, "You're forgetting that I have an internal compass, and I never get lost." It was true: he could travel to someplace one time and then be able to find it again five years later. The reminder comforted me, though his desire for another bachelor's degree or a pastor's job did not sit well.

When we were dating, we used to drive through the wealthier neighborhoods of our town, choosing homes that we liked. There was the Spanish-style home on South Main Street, with its dark brick and wrought-iron gate leading into an interior courtyard and garden. There were other, newer homes in the country club area, and we envisioned our future children playing there on wooden playsets with their brightly colored canopies. *This is what we wanted*, I thought as I fought back the tears. My vision for our life together was going to change.

Early the next spring, Craig received a phone call. It was from the dean of admissions, and he had a few questions about our finances. "We've saved $10,000," Craig told him, "plus we have no debt. As long as I can work part-time to pay for my schooling, my wife's job (when she gets one in California) will take care of our living expenses." By the time he got off the phone, he was accepted into the program as a married student, and we were headed to Southern California in three months.

Even Good People Suffer

I knew something was wrong when I read her rough draft discussing the effects of hunger: "Some people might wonder how hunger affects a person's intelligence. Children who are hungry at school can only think about the pain in their stomachs. They cannot pay attention in class, and this leads to bad grades." Norma's draft went on to elaborate about how both adults and children can be malnourished and susceptible to diseases because they cannot afford healthy food, and how the foods available at local food banks are often processed and high in sugar and salt.

Norma was part of a videoconferenced class that was connected to one of my face-to-face classes. She attended a satellite campus in a town about fifty miles away along with two other students. They watched my live lecture and interacted with the face-to-face class through a wide-screen TV. It was better than a strictly online class as it provided opportunities to ask questions, receive immediate answers, and clarify responses, but all the work was submitted online, and the satellite location did not offer extra support services.

She was older, with a disabled husband and two teenage sons, and she worked part-time at a nursing home as a State Tested Nursing Assistant (STNA), a certificate position lower in pay than a Licensed Practical Nurse (LPN), with hopes of becoming a Registered Nurse (RN) once she completed the nursing program. The rumblings of trouble started when her fourteen-year-old son became a father. His girlfriend was sixteen, and she already had an eighteen-month-old child with a different father. Norma wrote in her narrative, "I was afraid for my son and his future." After hearing the baby's heartbeat for the first time and seeing the ultrasound, she wrote that "Pure happiness took the place of that anger, fear, and grief that filled my heart. Though I was still afraid because my son was so young, too young to be a father, I knew my husband and I would do anything we could to help him and his new baby."

Being the family's sole source of income and going to school was hard on Norma, both mentally and physically.

A number of times she emailed that she was hospitalized overnight with heart issues and other health concerns which I assumed was due to stress from her son's situation. However, when I read the rough draft about the effects of hunger, I realized more was going on. Since she was in a town fifty miles away and the class was videoconferenced, I couldn't talk to her privately, but I could email her:

> Dear Norma,
>
> You said this topic of hunger was heartfelt, and I'm wondering if you are struggling and in need of economic support with essentials. I can check for you to see if we have anyone in the area that could help link you to support through a social service agency. Let me know.

While I waited to hear back from her, I also checked with our Success Center on the main campus to see if there was any help for situations like this. I knew we had a food pantry on campus, but unfortunately, no such support existed for students who attended satellite campuses miles away. The administrative assistant told me that other than seeing if financial aid (in the form of more student loans) was available, there were no other provisions in place for students struggling financially.

Later that day, Norma emailed me back: "Mrs. Kuhlman, it's true that my family is in financial trouble. Our house has been foreclosed on. We were living with the family of my fourteen-year-old son's girlfriend, but something happened. His girlfriend's mother decided we had to get out. She threw what little we had, our clothes, everything, out of the house. I was using their computer to do my homework, and my flash drive with my papers on it is still there. I don't know if I can get it back. I'll do my best to get my assignments to you." I felt sick to my stomach for Norma, for anyone who has been faced with hardship after hardship.

About a decade before, I had lived in the town where Norma was living, and my husband and I were well-acquainted with the director of the United Way. Though I wasn't sure if Deb was still the director there, I took a chance and called. We chitchatted and caught up, and then I told her about Norma. Deb said that due to factory closings and unemployment near ten percent, my student's situation was frequently the norm in the cases that she saw. "Local food banks, all three of them, are stretched, though the Salvation Army should be restocked due to the recent United Way Day of Caring food drive," Deb said. "But here's a bright spot. Tomorrow morning we will have the 211 service in town. This means that you can call 211 and confidentially/anonymously speak to someone who can guide you as far as support and aid available for your situation. Maybe she can talk to someone there."

I thanked Deb, grateful for any guidance I could get, and I emailed Norma back with the information. She still had access to her student email through her cell phone, and she wrote that she would call 211 the next day though she felt as if she were in a deep pit she could not climb out of: "I am spiraling into a deep depression, one I don't know if I can get out of. I have gone to the food banks, but with a family of teenage boys, it only lasts a couple days. I'm scared to take student loans to help in the meantime. I am trying to cope, to take it day by day, but the stress is overwhelming."

I read her response and felt helpless. I wanted to support Norma as she worked through these difficult situations that had nothing to do with academics, but I needed to maintain academic standards of integrity. Though I empathized with her, she still needed to complete the work to pass the class. The balance of empathy and academic rigor was my challenge; hunger and homelessness was hers. It seemed so unfair. I didn't know what she decided to do or how she pulled it together, but the assignments began to come in. They were adequate to pass the class, and I was not sure I could have done any better if I had been in her situation. From then on, whenever I read about how twelve percent of Ohioans are living in poverty,[5] and how cash payments such as welfare rarely lift these families out of poverty, I saw Norma's face.

---

[5] Ohio Development Services Agency. *The Ohio Poverty Report.* Columbus Office of Research, Feb. 2016, development.ohio.gov/files/research/p7005.pdf .

A Real Live Human

For our rural students like Norma, who would otherwise only have access to online classes, videoconferenced classes had become a staple. I became a regular teacher of these classes, which typically involved a face-to-face class with a camera and microphone that transmitted the lecture and class discussion to a TV in another classroom fifty miles away. Two or three students would meet in this off-campus classroom during our normal class time, and a camera and microphone on their end would allow me to involve them in the discussion and answer any questions they might have.

Joy was one of my off-campus students for a beginning composition course, and from the beginning, she struggled to understand the feedback I would provide on her written assignments. Luckily, she had a classmate at this satellite location who explained the assignment expectations and helped her understand where she was falling short, but even with this support, Joy barely made it through the class. As I graded her final assignment, I told her in my assessment that I wasn't confident that she completely grasped the basic concepts from the class. "If you need to take advanced composition," I wrote on her graded essay, "you must be sure to get a tutor from the very first day. Otherwise, you might not make it."

A year later I was reviewing my class lists for the new fall term when I saw Joy's name registered as an off-campus student for a videoconferenced class. *Oh, great,* I thought to myself. I doubted that she was prepared to take the class, and being off-campus greatly reduced her likelihood of securing a tutor. To make matters worse, she was the only student registered to take the class at the satellite campus.

The first assignment from her confirmed my fears. Her understanding of working with sources was still lacking, and since I couldn't speak with her privately in person, I emailed her:

Hi Joy,

As I communicated to you on the last graded assignment in our previous term together, I am not convinced that you have really grasped all the important concepts in Comp I. As you recall, the feedback I gave you on your last essay in Comp I said that if/when you sign up for Comp II, you will need a tutor and lots of support and motivation to get through. I don't know if tutoring is available to you at the satellite campus. If it isn't, I am worried that you will struggle. Last time, your classmate was a big support for you, but this time, you are by yourself. Though I know it is a drive, I recommend that you attend my face-to-face class so that you can use the Writing Lab and engage a tutor to sit with you as you put these assignments together. I still have room in my face-to-face class if you are able to do it. If not, you will need to find out what tutoring resources are available to you there.

Though I wasn't sure where she lived, I knew that for many of our students the reason they chose to attend a satellite campus was not because they enjoyed the videoconferenced format, but that it saved them gas money, an important concern when the lack of public transportation in rural areas required a car and the money to insure it and keep it running. I knew I was asking a lot, so I was surprised at her response:

Mrs. Kuhlman,

Thank you for your feedback. If there's room for me in your face-to-face class, I will come there if you think I would be better off.

Her willingness to come to the face-to-face class on the main campus gave me hope that she would be able to engage the tutor I was so certain she needed. The next Monday I met Joy face-to-face: brown curly hair, square dark frame glasses, and a ready smile. "It's so nice to see you in person, Joy," I told her with a smile. "I really appreciate you coming to the main campus. I know it must be a drive for you."

"It's actually not that much farther," Joy said, "so I only need to leave about fifteen minutes earlier." She shared how she was working part-time at a nursing home with the hope of getting her nursing degree. "I need to make it through Comp II as part of my degree program, so I'll be working extra hard for you."

"That sounds great. Don't forget to set up a tutor before the schedule is full," I suggested as I organized the class materials on my desk.

"Yep, I'll do that," Joy said as she took her seat at the back of the class. We began our discussion of the rhetorical analysis essay structure, and despite her seat in the back row, Joy seemed engaged in the class discussion.

I followed up with her a week or so later when our first major writing assignment was due. "So Joy, how's it going with the tutor?"

She shook her head. "I didn't get one. I think I understood the assignment, so I didn't feel like I needed the extra help."

Inwardly I cringed. I remembered her previous work from Composition I, and I could see no way that she could produce college-level writing. "What about the Writing Lab? They could help proofread for you."

"I used spell-check, and I tried reading my essay out loud like you said. It really helped. I think I'm good," Joy told me as she pulled out the final draft copy from her purple backpack.

I was doubtful, but I hoped my face didn't show it. I collected the final drafts from everyone and hoped for the best. Later that week, I made it through the pile of grading to Joy's manuscript. I read it through, and then I read it again. Though the pink pen in my hand was ready to mark errors, it remained at rest. Joy's paper was good, a far cry from what she had turned in during our last semester together.

I caught her after class the next time, having passed back the graded essays. "Joy, what great improvement you've shown in your writing!" I praised her.

Her brown eyes sparkled behind the dark frames, and she pushed her brown curls behind one ear. "I understand everything so much better in this face-to-face class," she shared. "In the other classroom, I had a hard time paying attention. I mean, it was like watching TV, and I could zone out."

"So you're not meeting with a tutor or having anyone help by reading your papers over?" I asked, skeptical that simply meeting in a face-to-face classroom could have such a profound effect.

"No, it really is just being in the classroom. That videoconferenced stuff is not for me, that much I can tell you," she said. "I need a person to talk to me, not someone on a TV."

"Keep it up," I encouraged her. "I am so proud of your efforts, Joy." Joy grinned as she left the classroom, and I paused to reflect on how I had misjudged her ability based on my experience with her in the satellite class. If I had misjudged Joy, who else might I be misjudging?

As the semester went on, Joy's assignments, both those written in class and those written outside of class, continued to reflect her improved understanding of academic writing and the use of sources. I was amazed to see how different her experience was between the two teaching venues. Though technology is often touted as a way to connect people, for Joy the technology got in the way. She needed a teacher "with skin on," not an image on a screen. And I was lucky enough to be that teacher.

Candy and Comfort

Margie freely admitted her age: fifty-five. I met her in a developmental class designed to boost the reading comprehension level of students, some of whom only could read at a fourth-grade level. Margie had a sixth-grade reading level, and she was pursuing a second career in criminal justice after the auto parts factory where she had worked for twenty-five years closed—another casualty of outsourcing. She was working at a gas station in addition to going to school, and her husband was a maintenance man/custodian for a parochial school in a nearby town.

We had a small group of seven in that class, six women ranging in age from eighteen to fifty-five, and one young man in his late teens. "Joe, do you know what some guys would do to be the only single man in the company of six beautiful women (well, seven, including me)?" I would tease him, and he would grin. It was this kind of rapport that helped make our daily work of vocabulary drills and rote memorization tolerable.

Unfortunately, taking tests was part of the syllabus, and I couldn't help but notice that Margie brought candy to class each time there was a test, sharing her treats with all of us. She had severe test anxiety, and she had heard that associating test-taking with something pleasant would help her deal with the anxiety better. The day of one of our chapter tests, comprised of multiple choice and true/false questions, I waited at the front of the classroom for everyone to finish. One by one, all the women and Joe completed their tests and left the room—except Margie.

She took a finger and wiped her eye and her cheek as she intently studied the paper. Ten minutes went by, and she still wrote nothing. Another finger wiped her eye again, and then another. I made my way to the back of the classroom where Margie sat, offering her a tissue. "What's wrong, Margie?"

"I've studied this stuff for a week, and I know it backward and forward until I get in the room. Then I forget everything." More tears rolled down her creased cheeks as her shoulders shook.

"What if I read the definitions or the questions to you?" I began to go through the test, focusing on the blanks remaining. She wiped her eyes and dried her glasses, slipping another Jolly Rancher cherry candy into her mouth. Before the class time ended, she had completed the test, and we both were laughing.

Margie knew she was really learning something in class, despite her struggles with test anxiety. In addition to our repetitious vocabulary work, we were reading *The Five People You Meet in Heaven* by Mitch Albom, working through its vocabulary in the context of the story about Eddie, an elderly amusement park worker who wrestles with whether or not his life has mattered to the world. When Eddie dies accidentally while saving a little girl at the park, he is shown bits of his life story from a broader perspective of several "guides," or people he knew long ago.

"I'm really liking this story," Margie shared with the class, the others nodding their heads in agreement. "Even if I don't know all the words, I like the idea of heaven and that your life has a deeper meaning than you realize. Even though my husband won't read, he likes me to tell him about it and what we talk about in class. He says he gets the nugget of the story without having to do the work!" she laughed, and we laughed with her.

"You should bring him to class with you sometime. If school is over at 3:00, he could make it here by our 4:00 class time," I encouraged.

Margie laughed. "He won't come, but even if he won't come and says he doesn't want to do the work, he's still learning! I just don't tell him that he's learning. Like the time I heard one of our vocabulary words on TV—what was it? Carnage—that was it! I was so excited! I told him I know what that means! So he says, 'Well, what does it mean?' and I said that carnage was a bloody mess!" Her enthusiasm for learning new words was contagious.

Despite the age difference, Margie made friends with the younger women in the class, and I often saw them eating lunch together or hanging out at the tables outside our classroom. From what I could observe, she offered them the mature wisdom of experience, free of judgment, and they gave her the hope of youth and the promise of a future. This promise turned out to be most important when her husband became ill.

After she missed a class or two, the other students passed along to me that Margie had taken her husband for some medical tests due to what she assumed was a urinary tract infection. The results were not good: stage four kidney cancer that was not curable but could be treated with radiation and chemotherapy. His treatments were scheduled at both the local hospital as well as the Cleveland Clinic, a good three hours away. Margie tried to keep up with her schoolwork, but as the middle of the term approached, she had to withdraw. "I couldn't juggle the doctors' appointments with work and school. I need to put my husband first, but I hope to be back next fall," she wrote optimistically in an email.

During the summer term, a little more than six months later, I ran into one of the six beautiful women who were part of that class. "How's Margie doing? Have you heard anything?"

The younger woman spoke, face fallen, "Margie's husband John died about a month ago. I don't know if she'll come back to school."

As I walked away, I thought about the word "carnage" and about Margie's life without her husband. I reached into my purse, and after groping around a little, I found a green apple Jolly Rancher. It had been in the bottom of my purse for a while, the once smooth wrapper wrinkled and dull. I reverently considered this candy and its ability to comfort by creating a pleasant physical sensation of sweetness. As I imagined the emotions of grief and loss Margie might be feeling, the same emotions I knew from other contexts, I offered her a prayer of solidarity with the rest of humanity who all suffer in one way or another. Almost like a ritual or an offering, I peeled away the sticky wrapper and popped the Jolly Rancher into my mouth. For Margie, for the new start she would have to make. For all of us, facing difficult endings and new beginnings.

Sandy Beaches and Shorts

Tears rolled down my cheeks as my husband and I sunbathed on the lovely Santa Monica Beach in Southern California. "Why can't you just enjoy the beach?" he asked. "We've only been here two days. You'll find a job once you have a chance to start looking."

I couldn't enjoy the sandy beach, the sunny sky, the salty smell of the ocean. All I could think about was finding a job. The thought rolled back and forth in my mind like the ocean waves crashing on the beach, and I remembered what it had taken to get us from Ohio to California. A few weeks before, we had moved into a nice apartment in Pasadena, California. We had enough saved to move us and meet three months of living expenses, and if I didn't find a job, we were headed home.

My work experience was in insurance, far, far away from my original dream of journalism and writing. Though I had dabbled in a bit of freelance writing for two local universities' alumni magazines, freelancing in the 1980s was difficult without the ease and opportunities of the internet. *Could I possibly break into a journalism job?* I would catch my breath at the thought. *Maybe this move will be my chance.*

The day after the crying-on-the-beach day, we needed to run errands: change drivers' licenses, buy a refrigerator, and switch our car and renters' insurance. After facing long lines at the Department of Motor Vehicles (known to Californians as "hell on earth") and picking out a fridge, we jotted down a few names of independent insurance agencies from the yellow pages to meet our third objective.

The first insurance agency was located on the third floor of a bank in downtown Pasadena. The waiting area was graced with fresh flowers from a local florist, and its décor was plush, speaking volumes about the wealthy clientele. I looked down at my wrinkled, gray cotton shorts, feeling a little underdressed. Just then an agent named Dan came out to see us.

We talked about the coverage we needed, and given my background at the insurance agency in Ohio, I was able to conversely knowledgeably. "You seem to know quite a bit about insurance," Dan said thoughtfully.

"I worked in personal insurance for an independent agent in Ohio the past few years," I told him.

Dan rubbed his chin. "Wait here a second," he said as he left our room. My husband and I looked at each other, wondering what was up. Would Dan have information about an insurance job somewhere?

My husband and I talked in low tones about this possibility while we waited. "I don't even know what a typical salary in California for an insurance clerk is," I thought aloud.

"Well, you made around $12,000 in Ohio, and our expenses have nearly tripled here, so I would ask for at least $30,000," he counseled.

"That seems pretty high for someone who only has two years of experience," I balked.

"Try it," my husband encouraged. "What do you have to lose?"

"I would sure feel better if I was asking for that much while I was wearing my suit," I muttered as I looked down again at the deep wrinkles crisscrossing the legs of my shorts.

After a few minutes, Dan returned. "Nan, would you be interested in a job as an insurance assistant here at our agency? We have an opening, and you would be working with another of our producers named Kate, dealing with her personal insurance customers and assisting another underwriter with Kate's commercial insurance clients."

"Yes, I would love that," I stammered, feeling as if I had broken the speed limit law and talked my way out of a ticket. Though I was elated at the prospect of employment, my hope of moving into a writing career was squashed.

"I'd like you to meet with a couple of my colleagues," Dan said as he motioned toward the door.

"But I'm not dressed appropriately for a job interview," I protested weakly, feeling more and more like I was facing a midterm I forgot to study for. "I don't even have a resumé."

"Oh, they won't care," he tossed over his shoulder as I followed him down the hallway. Dan introduced me to Kate, the salesperson I would be assisting. She glanced over the top of her half-reader glasses and motioned for me to sit down. "So it says here you've worked for an Ohio agency for two years?"

"Yes," I answered, sitting stiffly in an effort to look businesslike.

"What salary are you looking for?" Her eyes, dark and round, were no-nonsense as they studied me, shorts and all.

I took a breath and plunged. "Well, I made about $12,000 in Ohio, but with the cost of living out here, $30,000 might be more in line." My voice trailed off as she started to smirk.

"You're right that the cost of living is quite a bit higher here, but with only two years of experience, we wouldn't be able to offer $30,000. However, we pay a competitive wage for the market, probably more like $19,000."

My hope began to plummet. *I've blown it! Why did I ever say $30,000?* Just as I was ready to excuse myself and get out of there, she got up from her desk and motioned for me to follow. "Let's go meet the owners of the agency," she said as she led me back into the hallway.

Three interviews later, I actually believed that they didn't care that I was wearing wrinkled gray shorts. My husband joked that my great legs must have clinched the deal. I started my new job there the following Monday. Not a journalism job like I had hoped, but a job. With benefits. Another new start.

Chapter 3
Respecting Who You Are

Dreaming About Billing and Boundaries

I worked at the insurance agency handling a small book of personal insurance clients for my new boss, Kate, as well as supporting her commercial insurance underwriter. All of our client correspondence was via the US Postal Service — the internet and email were not used widely yet. Towards the end of each day, Kate meticulously reviewed each piece of mail, proofreading and checking for thoroughness, sometimes asking questions that led to more work, such as "Can you quote a few other companies for his auto insurance? I'm certain that we can do better than this." I would trudge back to my desk and redo the quotes, only to find out that what I originally offered was the best deal. This extra work wouldn't have been that bad except that Kate's commercial book of business was large, the largest in the office, and her underwriter Sunny and I were swamped with work.

Sunny was a force to be reckoned with. Looking like an African queen, she shared her story of making her way in Los Angeles after moving there from Texas, dabbling in modeling before landing in the insurance business. When I asked why she left Texas, she told me she had fallen in love with a sailor who was white and became pregnant before he decided that the next port was calling him. Her pregnancy was fraught with difficulty, and she delivered her daughter prematurely. After a few years of struggle, both economically and socially, Sunny decided to move to Southern California, a place where mixed ethnicities abounded. She hoped it could be a place where her daughter would not be ostracized for being bi-racial.

"I thought that it was against the law to discriminate," I said naively, not understanding that legislation wouldn't change deeply-held narratives.

"There are towns in Texas," she told me, "where no Black person should ever stop to get gas. Even after Martin Luther King, Jr., and the civil rights movement, it's still that way today."

I shook my head in amazement, mistakenly believing that issues of race were simply historical memories from the 1960s, not a part of the late 1980s. My rural northwestern Ohio upbringing had fed me a homogenous soup that kept me from seeing the problems people of color faced. My school district in the 1970s, which encompassed eight different zip codes, only had two

African-American families. As I reflected on the way these two students, one boy and one girl, navigated our high school, I realized that they were confined through unspoken rules to dating other black students from other high schools. Interracial dating had not been an issue, perhaps because no one wanted to be different but maybe also because we, too, were deeply steeped in the narrative about the importance of maintaining an ethnic separation. More than a decade later, I could see more clearly the thread of racism even where I thought it had been uprooted.

Sunny was a good teacher, not just in the field of commercial insurance but in understanding people. She would sit with me as I called company underwriters, presenting a commercial risk that I needed to find coverage for. After saying hello and identifying myself, I launched into my description of the risk, trying to minimize what I knew they wouldn't like and emphasize what I thought they would. More times than I could count, the underwriter would graciously decline. "What am I doing wrong?" I asked in frustration.

"You're forgetting that underwriters are people first, underwriters second," Sunny told me. "You need to talk to them like people, find out about them, and be interested in what they're doing outside of work." I was taken aback by Sunny's advice: I was trying so hard to be professional, forgetting that business people are people who work to support themselves and their families. Sometimes they loved their work, and sometimes they didn't. I was more than an insurance underwriting assistant; the people I was speaking with were also much more than their business title. I found this revelation freeing in that I could ask questions and express interest in the people I worked with over the phone. I soon found out that I relished learning what my business contacts did over the weekend and how their day was going. Being human and interested in other humans made insurance work more bearable.

Though I quickly learned many of the finer points of business insurance coverage and how to market business risks to companies, we could not keep up with all the work Kate's burgeoning commercial accounts required. At the end of each week, we counted our "backlog," the number of pieces of mail we did not touch or process. This was an office practice, one that everyone had to complete before leaving for the weekend, and its intent supposedly was to help management know where to schedule additional part-timers to work during the next week. For me, though, the backlog was a source of stress. I had been raised that before you "played," you finished your work. The problem with that philosophy was that it didn't work in this job. Sunny and I couldn't keep up with over four hundred business accounts (plus my personal lines accounts, which numbered less than one hundred).

"We're going to get fired, Sunny," I would say as I finished the count of over a hundred pieces of backlog. I needed my job; Craig was still a student and only working part-time.

"We're not going to get fired," Sunny would say confidently. "Who they goin' to get to do the work?"

There was a certain logic to that, and I knew that Kate considered Sunny a skillful marketer and a competent underwriter. My status in Kate's eyes was still questionable since I was reasonably new and unproven. At night I would dream of billing clients and completing applications and other correspondence, Kate's scowl morphing into other unknown faces of disapproval. "Faster, faster!" she would say with the chorus of naysayers, looking over the top of glasses and down her nose at me. "If you can't do the work, we'll have to get someone who can!" When I woke the next day to go to work, I felt as if I had never left.

Dudes and Devotion

I was subbing for a colleague when I met Michael in a developmental writing class. His black beanie and monochromatic clothes matched his speech: "And I was like, whoa, dude, step back." He was cool, rad, righteous, rufus, and all the other positive, modern slang adjectives you might think of.

During one of our class times together, Michael asked me to help him after class with one of his rough drafts.

"Like I know what I want to say," he said, "but like what I put down on paper doesn't sound right."

I took a look at what he had, and his writing looked something like this:

"The best yaw ot be successful in college si to study harb."

"Michael, do you have dyslexia?" I asked him.

"Yeah, like I've always had trouble spelling and reading and stuff. Most of the time I can see mistakes if I read through it again. Guess those ones got away from me," he grinned, completely at ease with himself and his learning disability. He corrected the errors in the sentence without any help from me, and we continued through his draft.

The assignment focused on what it takes to be successful at anything, and as I read on through Michael's paper, I was surprised. I felt like I was working with a cross between a friend of Bill and Ted from the movie *Bill and Ted's Excellent Adventure* and the Buddha. Sentences like "Working hard in any job or class is important, but at the end of the day, a person cannot control everything" made me take a sideways glance at the young man beside me.

I read on: "A person, no matter what job they work, has to learn that life is not about controlling everything but learning to roll with what life brings. Life constantly changes, so we can't expect the good times to go on forever. The good news on the flip side of this is that the bad times don't last either."

"Wow," I said, more to myself than to Michael.

"Is that a good 'Wow' or a bad 'Wow?'" he asked.

"It's good, it's deep, and it's thoughtful," I told him. "Where did you learn to think about life this way at your age?"

He paused, scratching his head under the black beanie. "I don't know. I listen to a lot of podcasts when I'm working or driving. There are some great ones out there, Mrs. K. You should check 'em out."

After I wrote down a few podcast recommendations, we finished polishing up his draft. He picked up his backpack, sliding the straps over one shoulder first then the other. "See you next time, Mrs. K," he called as he headed out the door, carrying a skateboard under his arm. I glanced out the window as I packed my bag, to see him on the skateboard in the parking lot, weaving in and out of the parked cars.

Once I finished subbing for that class, a year or so passed before I ran into Michael again at the beginning of fall semester. This time we both were waiting to talk to the dean of the Arts & Sciences division. "So Michael, how have you been?"

Still wearing a black beanie, Michael replied, "Not bad. Ready to get back to school."

"Did you ever take Composition I?" I asked, and when he nodded his assent, I followed up. "How'd it go?"

"Mrs. K, I had a really great teacher. If I did bad on an assignment, she let me redo it. I think I ended up with a B.

But man, that was a lot of writing. I'm glad to be done with that!"

"So what did you do this summer? Did you work a lot?"

"Yeah, I worked for my dad. He's a house painter, and this summer we were really busy. My grandma never knew when I was going to be home, and she said she was getting tired of eating alone. She's glad I'm back at school now."

We commiserated over the hassles of painting a house, as I had just painted the entire interior before we moved into our new house. Then I asked, "Do you live with your grandmother, Michael?"

"My parents divorced a long time ago and never got along, so I've always lived with my grandma. She's not doing as good as she used to these days. Kinda has me worried."

"You take care of her then?"

"Yeah, but she took care of me since I was little. Taught me manners and all. She made me open doors and even the car door for her. Said she was training me to be a gentleman. Now I always do that, so I guess her training took!" Michael sat back with a satisfied look on his face.

"Your grandmother sounds like she is a great lady." I noticed his eyes beginning to tear up.

"She's the best. She always tells me I can do whatever I put my mind to. I don't want to paint houses forever, even though I make pretty good money. I want to work on computers and help people. I think that working on computers is a way of helping people, don't you think, Mrs. K?"

"Absolutely," I said, sharing the number of times I relied on tech support to talk me off a cliff over a seemingly unsolvable computer issue. The secretary came out to tell Michael that the dean was free to see him. He turned to me, tipped his beanie in respectful acknowledgment, and said, "It was a pleasure chatting, Mrs. K."

As he traipsed back into the dean's office, I thought of a line from *Bill and Ted's Excellent Adventure:*

> Bill: "So-cratz [says] 'The only true wisdom consists in knowing that you know nothing.'"
>
> Ted: "That's us, dude."[6]

That's me, too, Michael. I'm forever learning to respect the breadth and depth of the human heart.

———————————✳———————————

Older, Not Always Wiser

I once read in the community college catalog that senior citizens (those over the age of sixty) could enroll in classes free of instructional fees as long as they were state

---

[6] "Quotes – Bill & Ted's Excellent Adventure." IMDb.com, imdb.com/title/tt0096928/quotes.

residents for at least a year, though lab and book fees still applied. This pleased me, because I'm a believer in lifelong learning. As is often the case, though, practical experience can challenge abstract beliefs, and my experience with Catherine and Betty showed me the wide dichotomy that can exist in older learners.

Catherine was in a summer advanced composition class. This meant that she (and her classmates) had to cover a typical sixteen-week semester's worth of material and assignments in an accelerated eight-week term. Though it was a rigorous exercise, Catherine was up for it, having attended college almost forty years before.

"What was your bachelor's degree in?" I asked her one day during a break.

"It was computer programming. They called it 'Management Information Systems' at the time, and the computers we worked on filled an entire room," Catherine said with a grin, shaking her head, her long, waist-length gray hair moving from side to side. She reminded me of a hippie from the 1970s with that long gray hair, loose blouses and jeans, and warm smile.

"Why are you coming back to school at a community college? I asked. "I would think that you'd want to pursue a master's or an advanced degree."

"Well, it's been so long since I've been in school that I felt like I should review some. I mainly just wanted to learn, and with the free classes for senior citizens, I could pick up an associate's in math and maybe work into a different career."

This piqued my interest. "So you're retired?" Her blue eyes behind the large, plastic-rimmed eighties glasses crinkled as she nodded. "Let's just say I retired a little early from a university near here after having worked in their IT department for over thirty years. I have my retirement savings; now I can learn something new."

Something new included academic writing, and Catherine expressed some concern about her ability to write, especially after so many years away from it. "You know, I think the standards were a little lower back in the day," she confided one day during a break. "I mean, we had to write papers, but our sources came from our university library, and we weren't expected to figure out what were reliable or authoritative sources. Even though we have so much more information available now, it seems like it has just complicated everything."

I agreed, and I told her that she had nothing to worry about with respect to academic writing. Catherine was bringing her years of life experience to her writing and that would more than make up for the decades during which she wrote nothing at all.

One day in class we were discussing an essay by second-wave feminist Germaine Greer, called "One Man's Mutilation is Another Man's Beautification."[7] "I remember

---

[7] Greer, Germaine. "One Man's Mutilation Is Another Man's Beautification." *The Millennium Reader,* edited by Stuart Hirschberg and Terry Hirschberg, Pearson Education, Inc., 2009, pp. 682-690.

her," Catherine said. "She wrote *The Female Eunuch* back in the 70s. That book was all the rage in the dorms as I remember."

Greer's essay sparked discussion, particularly on the issue of tattoos. The essay was an excerpt from a work written originally in the mid-1980s, and views about tattoos had changed dramatically during those three decades since. Catherine seemed intrigued by Greer's take on tattoos. "I think Greer's work is somewhat prophetic," she said. "Look at what she says here: 'We are on the brink of an era in which most people will be condemned to a life of enforced leisure and mere subsistence. It may very well be that these displacement activities [such as tattoos] will have to evolve into legitimate art forms involving a strong and healthy body decorated with skill, sophistication, and meaning.'[8] This sounds like she saw how tattoos would become a way of self-expression and a method of creating meaning, even though she wrote this about thirty years ago."

I could see the younger students, especially those with tattoos, nodding their heads and reading Greer's words with new appreciation. While I could have pointed out the same thing, it made such a difference to have a student, one of their own (albeit a little older), show them the intricacies of an older written work that offered perspective on a current cultural trend.

---

[8] Ibid, 690.

I ran into Catherine again a couple of years later. She told me she had met her original goal of earning her associate's degree in math, but she was enjoying tutoring students in math and composition, so she decided to take more classes to continue doing that. "I take some computer classes on Mondays and Wednesdays," she told me, "and on Tuesdays and Thursdays I tutor students all day long. I really enjoy it."

She looked good, her waist-length gray hair now chopped off to shoulder-length, but still parted in the middle à la 1970s Joan Baez, and newer, updated glasses accenting her keen blue eyes. She was wearing a brown herringbone blazer with her jeans, and I couldn't help thinking that she looked like a university professor from the 1980s. I felt good knowing that students had the support and wisdom of someone like Catherine. Though culture had changed, some things remained constant.

Around the same time I met Catherine, I began tutoring students individually. My first student was Mary Black, according to the appointment schedule. We were to meet twice a week for one hour to work on beginning composition, and on our first scheduled appointment I showed up at the tutoring center. No Mary. I waited for five minutes or so, chatting with the receptionist when a petite, older woman with bleached blond hair came rushing up. Her face was heavily lined with age and her eyes seemed to focus somewhere besides the face of the person she was speaking to.

"I'm sorry I'm late," she said breathlessly. "I've been trying to locate a table where I can plug in my laptop because the battery is almost dead. By the way, I'm Betty," she said, offering a hand.

"Hi, Betty," I said, shaking her hand. "I thought your name was Mary, but you go by Betty?"

Betty laughed, "Yes, I'm Mary Elizabeth, but I answer to Betty."

"Well, Betty, if your laptop is dead, let's go find a computer in the library where we can look at your beginning composition assignment." We walked down the hallway to the library and found a computer and an extra chair available. "Do you have your document on a flash drive, Betty?"

"Actually, I haven't started it yet," she said as she sat down, rummaging through her bag to find an elusive flash drive.

As we talked about her assignment, which was a narrative showing how her perspective of the world changed based on a particular experience, I learned about Betty's decision to go back to school under the senior citizens' free tuition plan. "I always tell my husband Carl that you're never too old to learn something," she said. "I wanted him to go back to school with me, but he said he'll just come with me and read the newspaper in the library while I go to classes."

"What do you want to major in?" I asked.

"Accounting, I'm pretty sure. I like numbers," Betty said as she fumbled with the computer keyboard. "Now, where do we go to create a document?"

I began to show her the basics of setting up an MLA-formatted Word document, and with each step, Betty exhibited so much surprise and elation as her document began to look like the sample her instructor had provided. I enjoyed her "oohs" and "aahs" because most of the time, my students knew more about Word software than I did.

Betty began to work on a family story about a childhood fight with her sister, and how her father mediated the situation between them. We made sure she had a good thesis statement, and when I left her, she was ready to continue telling her story with our next meeting scheduled in two days. I felt good when I left her, certain that progress was being made.

We met again on Tuesday, and I was excited to see what she had added to her narrative. "Hi, Betty," I said as I sat down at her table in the students' common area. There was an older man reading a newspaper with her. "Are you Carl?" I asked.

He smiled and gave a deep chuckle that seemed to bubble up from within. "Yes, yes, I am," he said as he shook my hand. Carl's eyes were kind, and as he rose to his feet, I noticed he moved slowly, deliberately, as if he had all the time in the world. "Well, I'll be leaving you two to get that schoolwork done," he said as sauntered toward the library, still carrying a section of the newspaper with him.

Betty plugged in her flash drive, and then she began to look for her narrative document. "Well, I thought I put it here," she said, clicking on an icon. "Nope, that isn't it." She clicked on a number of them before she finally landed on the right document. "I still need to add some more to it," she said, "but I think I have it pretty much done."

I stared at the document. The MLA formatting was gone. The introduction and the thesis statement we worked on together last time—gone. "Betty, what happened to the formatting we did last time and the introduction?" I could barely contain my exasperation.

"I don't know," Betty said. "I thought it looked a little different when I opened it up after our meeting, but I wasn't sure." Her face fell, and I immediately felt contrite that I had raised the issue.

"It's OK," I tried to sound upbeat. "We'll just have to do it again. When did you say this final draft was due?"

"Tomorrow," Betty offered, "but my instructor said I could turn it in a little late since I was getting help from a tutor."

Together we worked on restoring her formatting, rewriting her thesis statement, and smoothing out her wording for her narrative. The hour went by quickly, but before I left, I made sure she saved the document and made a mental note which folder on her flash drive held it.

The following week Betty was ecstatic. "You're not going to believe it!" she said as she planted her paper in front of me. "I got an A!"

I congratulated her for her effort, but in the back of my mind, I was thinking that the narrative is the easiest assignment in beginning composition. Its purpose is to help beginning writers understand the importance of an introductory paragraph with a thesis statement and a separate conclusion paragraph. Even though she received an A, I wasn't convinced that Betty understood the big takeaways of introductions with thesis statements and a separate conclusion. I had a sense that despite her enthusiasm and love of learning, retention might be an issue.

We began working on her next assignment, and though we had covered MLA formatting a couple of times, Betty still showed genuine amazement as her document took shape. "It looks like a real paper," she said, eyes wide and childlike. She patted a thick library book that was lying on the table. "I have to use this book from the library as a source, so I'm going to need help putting it on a works cited page."

"No problem," I assured her. "We'll do the works cited page first, and then get you started with your introduction and thesis statement." We worked for a while, and Betty was so sweet and appreciative. After carefully saving her document, I told her, "Now you are all set to finish it before our next meeting, right?"

She assured me she would, and right on schedule, Carl came around the corner, carrying his newspaper. "I think Betty is going to be busy writing this weekend, Carl. Don't distract her too much," I joked, just to hear his bubbly laugh.

Carl obliged. "You don't have to worry about me," he said with his deep, smiling voice. "As long as I have my paper," and he waved it in Betty's face.

"Oh, Carl," she responded with mock consternation. "That's all you do—read newspapers."

"Yeah, and all you do is write papers. I think I got the better deal," he laughed, and I laughed too, appreciating his calm, centered joviality. The two gathered Betty's book bag and laptop bag, and they headed toward the parking lot, Carl with his smooth, tall, unhurried gait and Betty beside him, taking three steps for each one of his.

Later that week my daughter and I were grocery shopping when I turned our cart into the next aisle only to see Betty and Carl coming toward us. "Mrs. Kuhlman," Betty said as she came over beside me, "do you know shorthand?"

"No, Betty, I don't. I don't even think anybody uses shorthand any more."

"Well, my sister-in-law gave me this list of things she wanted me to pick up, and I can't make out this one item. I thought maybe she was writing in shorthand."

I looked closely at the list where she pointed. "It looks like the word 'smokes' to me, but I'm not sure."

"Oh, yes," she said. "Carl, she wants us to get her cigarettes, not those little smokey sausages. Now why in the world didn't she just write cigarettes? Thanks, Mrs. Kuhlman. Carl, where are you going? We've got to get those smokes." Betty chased Carl down the aisle as he ambled over to the Little Debbie snacks.

The grocery store incident foreshadowed the difficulties to come at our next meeting and every meeting after that. During our next appointment, Betty opened her document only to find all the formatting and all the work we did together had vanished. In its place was a hodge-podge of sentences, most with the depth of a kiddie pool. After we worked to reconstruct her essay again, I vented to a colleague in private: "I've just been 'Betty-ed.' It's like that movie *50 First Dates* where every morning Drew Barrymore's character wakes up to relive the same day over and over. Or *Groundhog Day*, except that Bill Murray at least made progress as he relived the day over and over. He learned to play the piano, for cryin' out loud. Betty can't seem to keep her margins the same from paper to paper, and there's a default setting for that! It's a good thing she's going into accounting."

"I doubt she'll make it through accounting. I think she's taken developmental math twice already," my colleague said, shaking her head.

I understood then that this was not the typical tutoring job, one where both student and tutor could see progress made. Lifelong learning is a deeply-held value for me, and I remember as a college student firmly believing in anyone's ability to earn a college degree with enough hard work. My youthful optimism was being tempered with maturity and real life experience as I realized that for some, there are limits to their ability to learn.

Each time we met and she opened her document, I cringed to see what was left of the work we did. Yet each time we worked to restore her formatting and create some order out of the chaos, Betty was so appreciative. "Oooh, that looks so nice," she would say as she looked my way. "I'm so glad I have you as a tutor."

My face reddened as we turned our attention to fixing what was in front of us. *Why couldn't she just get it? She's going to make me look bad.* My own thoughts stopped me at that moment. I only wanted to tutor someone who would get better, someone that I could say I had a hand in helping succeed. *What kind of teacher is that?* Though I considered myself the champion of the underdog, those "underdogs" always had something on the ball, something I could work with and build on. Not Betty. For whatever reason, she wanted to try to learn. And all I had to do was encourage without putting my baggage on her.

"Everyone is your teacher," I had heard before, but I had never had a teacher like Betty. Once I let go of my expectations about her progress, I was able to spend that hour with her, attending to her questions and concerns without attaching my ego's need to share in her success. We met twice a week for practically the entire term, but she still failed beginning composition.

The last time I saw Carl and Betty was again at the grocery store. They didn't see me, mostly because Betty had spilled her Pepsi on the floor at the exit of the store, and Carl was crouched down, trying to wipe it up with paper towels, dodging the automatic doors as they swung back and forth. Betty stood there with the cart of groceries, eyes unfocused, oblivious to the crowd of people who waited behind her, trying to leave the store and move forward in life.

<hr />

The Voice of Experience

"I'm more of a numbers person, not a writer," Evelyn told me on the first day of our class. She had an East Coast accent, I noticed, so I mentioned it and asked where she was born. "Massachusetts," she said proudly, glad that it was still obvious to others despite her years of living in Ohio. The rest of class had left the room, and so I asked her about why she was in school. I was curious because she was clearly near retirement age.

"I was a scheduler for an in-home caregiver company. I worked my way up, starting as an LPN and taking care of senior citizens. Right before I was laid off, I wrote the new compliance manual and nursing protocol to meet state regulatory mandates. Then the owner sold the business, and the new management decided they didn't need me," she said with her eyes narrowed and brows furrowed, deepening the crease between. "So glad I could help out," she mimicked sarcastically, the heavy smog of bitterness palpable in the air. "I only needed three more years to be eligible for social security, but they couldn't keep me on," she shook her head, still wrestling with how a business could make a decision that upends a faithful employee's life.

Along with writing the compliance manual for the business, Evelyn told me about how she created a schedule where everyone worked the same days with the same shift each week, and how the staff loved having a regular schedule they could count on. She shook her head. "I work at Walmart now, and I could teach them a thing or two about scheduling. I never know from week to week what days I'm going to work there."

"Why do you say you're not a writer if you wrote the compliance mandates and nursing protocol to satisfy the state?"

She shrugged her shoulders, her matronly build accentuated by the loose blouse she wore over equally loose khaki pants, and then ran a hand over her short graying hair. "I don't see why I have to learn how to write academic papers if I'm training to go into accounting."

"So it's not that you're not a writer; it's just that you don't like to write and don't know why you have to take classes in it?"

"Writing, at least this academic writing we're doing, has nothing to do with accounting. I don't understand why I have to do all this work and pay money for writing classes when in accounting I'm only going to be dealing with numbers," Evelyn said with some impatience, as if she had said something similar to other administrators and it had fallen on deaf ears. "Everyone tells me that it is a state-driven requirement, something about helping students 'round out' their education." She rolled her eyes.

Rather than try to justify my class as a requirement, I gave her a safe answer: "I don't know." This was not the first time I had heard this viewpoint from students who wanted to get out of taking my class. Any time I tried to explain the importance of writing as part of a "well-rounded" education to my older students, they would look at me sideways and respectfully say, "Mrs. Kuhlman, I don't need to be 'well-rounded.' I'm fifty-nine years old. I need a job." I realized my typical response was something that college administrators might say, thinking they were equipping students with much-needed critical thinking skills. My older students, in most cases, were the best critical thinkers I had in class; I couldn't dispute their logic.

Evelyn rarely answered questions in class unless called upon, yet her homework assignments revealed that she had a good comprehension of the reading assignments. "Why don't you answer questions in our class discussion, Evelyn?" I asked her after class one day. "I know you know the material—what's up?"

She sniffed, reminding me of a British nanny I'd seen on TV. "These young kids—they don't think older students like me know anything." She seemed defiant in her response, and I wondered if she had been treated disrespectfully in another class.

"I think they listen to you more than you realize," I tried to reassure her. After that, I made an effort to call on her in class as her responses were always well-thought-out, though she offered them as if she expected the other students to argue or disagree with her. They never did.

Three of the other students in the class were nursing students from a nearby four-year college who were taking advanced writing composition at our community college as part of a deal worked out between the two colleges. They were excellent writers, yet I overheard them talking nervously about the nursing protocol project, a twenty-page document they had to write as their final project to receive their nursing degree.

"Did you know that Evelyn has written a nursing protocol before? She used to work for an in-home caregiving agency, and she wrote the protocol to satisfy the state mandates," I told them within Evelyn's earshot. "You should ask her about it."

I had some graded papers to hand back at the beginning of class, and as I did that, I heard the nursing students talking to Evelyn. "So how'd you know what to write? It seems so overwhelming."

"Yeah," said another. "I was thinking of changing my major because I didn't know if I could do it. What if I missed something important?" She slumped back in the chair, defeated before she had even tried.

Evelyn sat up straight, shoulders back, and said, "It wasn't that hard. Just look at it as having to write a bunch of two-page papers and address each heading as a separate paper." She went on, the young nursing students engrossed in what she was sharing, even taking notes. I took my time handing back graded papers that day as I watched Evelyn soak up the rays of respect from those nursing students like a plant kept too long in the dark reaching for sunlight.

Writing for Life

I learned from my work in insurance that you can be good at something, receiving respect and accolades from your colleagues, and not really enjoy it. This surprised me, I think, because I enjoy being successful—who doesn't? Yet within that success, there was something lacking, and I began to look for it during my lunch hour.

I had left my job assisting Sunny for a higher-paying job at another insurance agency, this time in South Pasadena. The South Pasadena Library, originally a Carnegie library built in 1908, was a block away from the new insurance agency where I worked. It offered books and an inviting place to sit outside under a jacaranda tree that bloomed with light purple blossoms at certain times of the year. I ate my packed lunch there often, enjoying crisp salads with black and green olives and lots of homegrown California avocado as I dabbled in poetry or drawing.

Writing the Natural Way: Using Right-Brain Techniques to Release Your Expressive Powers was one of the library books I used for these lunchtime practices. Author Gabriele Lusser Rico writes about using various techniques to see (with the help of the right side of the brain) more nuances connecting the reader to the author's purpose, and she shares the following quote from writer Anaïs Nin: "We...write to heighten our own awareness of life...We write to taste life twice, in the moment and in retrospection...We write to be able to transcend our life, to reach beyond it...to expand our world when we feel strangled, constricted, lonely...When I don't write I feel my world shrinking."[9]

I felt my world shrinking as I made money in the insurance business. The talk of liability, pricing, and coverage wrapped around my throat like a boa constrictor, so I began to think about my escape. My husband, having completed his second bachelor's in theology, was working in wealth management at a well-known bank in Beverly Hills. His dream was to be a pastor or counselor or both,

[9] Rico, Gabriele Lusser. Writing the Natural Way: Using Right-Brain Techniques to Release Your Expressive Powers. St. Martin's Press, 1983, p. 11.

but the opportunities were not there when he graduated. So he went back into banking, rubbing shoulders with celebrities and millionaires during the day and then coming home to our one-bedroom apartment in Pasadena. He also was planning his escape, or at least he was making himself ready by taking classes at California State University, Los Angeles (Cal State LA) and working toward a master's in marriage and family counseling.

It was fall, the time of year when a person who likes school starts to think about going to school again, and with my husband already going to Cal State LA, I started to research at the South Pasadena Library the English majors they offered. Though I already had a bachelor's in journalism, I knew I didn't want to be a reporter anymore. I liked the regular hours of insurance, so I began to think about what I could do with a master's degree in English.

"You could teach," my husband said to me as we surveyed the course catalog. I had never considered teaching at the post-secondary level. I studied the courses offered in the Master of Arts in English program: British lit, ancient lit, American lit, multi-cultural studies, creative writing.

"I could teach," I said, feeling hopeful and full of possibilities. The tightness in my throat began to loosen as I started to complete my application to attend night classes at Cal State LA. My husband and I could plan to go to school there the same nights so I wouldn't be traveling alone after dark. I sent my application in to begin in the January term, and then I waited.

My acceptance arrived in the mail the beginning of December, but along with it was a requirement to provide proof of having been vaccinated for measles, mumps, and rubella (MMR). Though I had all the typical immunizations, the last MMR shot I'd received had been more than twenty years before, so I had to be immunized again and provide proof before I could register.

I scrutinized the calendar closely. My monthly period was a little late, an oddity for me since my cycle ran like clockwork. *Could I be pregnant?* At first, I didn't think it could be possible, and then I remembered one time…*No way! I'm twenty-nine years old, so I'm probably not as fertile as someone younger. Surely it would take more than once.*

"So when are you going to see the doctor to get immunized?" my husband asked, oblivious to my thoughts. "You don't have much time to register for January classes."

"Well, there might be a slight problem. Not a bad problem, a good problem," I tried to sound reassuring as I processed the possibility of pregnancy myself. "I can't get the MMR vaccine until I know for sure that I'm not pregnant."

"Pregnant?" My husband practically spat the word out of his mouth.

"Well, you remember that one time…" I reminded him.

"Oh, yeah, but that was just one time," he said, rationalizing that the "one time" could not possibly result in a pregnancy for a nearly thirty-year-old.

"I know. But I can't get the vaccine until I know for sure because it can cause birth defects if you get it when you're pregnant," I told him.

"When are you going to get one of those early pregnancy tests?" he asked, clearly a little shaken by the possibility of impending fatherhood.

"Tomorrow. We should know by the next morning," I said with more confidence than I actually felt.

I bought the test at the pharmacy the next day, feeling more like a schoolgirl in trouble than a mature woman who had been married for five years. The next morning I peed in the cup, put the stick in the pee, and watched as the blue plus sign became bluer and bluer.

"Yep," my husband said. "We got a bun in the oven." His shock was overcome with male pride, pleased that he had been able to procreate and continue the species.

"Yes," I said as I kissed him. Fears about pregnancy and parenthood quickly replaced my dreams of creative writing and a master's degree in English. I had been practicing the writing during my lunches at the South Pasadena Library, but I had no plan for practicing how to be a good mother, though my own mother was a good example. A new season required a new plan.

Chapter 4
Moving Through Seasons

Moving Back Home

The news showed plumes of smoke rising from southcentral Los Angeles. It was the end of April 1992, and the police officers who had beaten an African-American man, Rodney King, a year before, had just been acquitted of wrongdoing. Riots and looting began in response, and while I was tucked away in Pasadena, my husband, who worked in Beverly Hills for a bank, called me to say the bank was closing and sending its employees home, fearful that the rioters would venture toward the luxury shops of Rodeo Drive just a couple miles down the road.

On the following Saturday, we were walking together on our shady route through the well-heeled homes of San Marino near The California Institute of Technology. My husband wanted to have five years of big city wealth management experience on his resumé before returning to our home state of Ohio, but with a baby due in just a little less than four months, he was concerned about safety and our ability to make it on just his income.

"You know, I could call my old boss Joe Vlaskowitz just to let him know I might be interested in something in the next couple of years," he said.

"Yeah, but if he has something available now, you'll have to take it. If you turn it down, you'll have used your trump card," I told him as I rubbed my lower abdomen where the baby was kicking.

"You're right," he conceded, and we continued our walk through San Marino, stopping briefly to watch a movie crew film a scene for a soon-to-be-released Eddie Murphy movie called *The Distinguished Gentlemen*.

A few days later at his office, my husband had an overwhelming urge to call his former boss Joe. He picked up the phone. "Hey, Joe, it's Craig Kuhlman here. How are things in Ohio?" They chitchatted about family happenings and people they knew, and then Craig asked if Joe had heard of any openings in banking in northwest Ohio.

"Actually," Joe began, "we're about three days out from advertising a trust position in Lima. Are you interested?"

Within a week or so, we were flying back to Ohio to visit family, but also to have Craig interview for the open position. He landed the job, and within two months we were moving home.

Though home meant Ohio, it also meant moving in with my in-laws. With starting a new job and a new baby arriving in less than two months, Craig did not want to look for an apartment in Lima. The plan was to live with his parents until after the baby was born, and then we would look for a place of our own.

His parents, though glad to have us back, had little room to spare in their thousand-square foot home. Our room was a small bedroom, and the closet was half full of too-small clothes from the both of them, neatly hung and covered with plastic. We had to put our clothes on a bookshelf that we cleared of books, stacking them under the bed and under the hand-me-down crib my mother-in-law had bought for $10 at a garage sale. Space was like breathable air, and I gulped for it like a deep-sea diver returning to the surface. I longed for my own place, and my own belongings. I was in limbo: not working yet not a mother, back in Ohio but not really home. Even their Yorkshire terrier seemed to want us to leave, pooping in our bedroom any time we left the door open. The confinement made me claustrophobic and caustic, sometimes wounding the gentle spirit of my mother-in-law who loved to have an abundance of knick-knacks and mementos around.

Needing to feel useful, I was cooking dinner for everyone, and the inexpensive figurines on the countertop were sitting in way of my cooking process. One in particular that irritated me, a cheap frog on a lily pad holding a sign that said, "You would be happy, too, if you could eat what bugs you."

What bugs me is you, I thought to myself as I tossed the ceramic figure into the drawer and then devoted my attention to finishing dinner.

Later that evening, my mother-in-law was wiping the counter down as we cleaned up the dishes. "Where's my frog?" she asked.

"I may have put it in the drawer to get it out of the way when I was cooking," I said lamely.

She looked in the drawer and pulled it out. "Oh, it's broken!" she said as if it was more than just a cheap figurine. "Craig got me this for my birthday when he was ten, and he had just started the paper route." She attempted to put the broken lily pad leaf back in place, without success. "Guess I should just throw it away," she said as she carefully placed it in the wastebasket.

I wanted to defend my actions. I mean, the house was cluttered, and I did need some space to work on dinner. But seeing her face made me realize that this clutter was more than just things—it was memories. It was time in a bottle—or in a ceramic figurine of a frog. Each item or article of clothing held special memories that would be lost to her or at least dishonored if that item were thrown away. Though I didn't realize it at the time, it foreshadowed her decline into Alzheimer's, when even the tangible items themselves were no longer enough to hold on to the memories.

I apologized for putting the frog in the drawer, and said, "I feel like I'm without a home, without a place of my own right now. I miss having my own space." Tears filled my eyes, and she nodded her assent though I'm not completely sure she understood.

Less than two months after we arrived in Ohio, our first son was born. "What will you call him?" my OB-GYN Dr. Patel asked with his thick accent.

"His name is Quentin," I responded, probably with a thick accent of unknown origin, stemming from thirteen hours of labor that ended in a C-section.

"Clinton? Oh, you must be voting Democrat this election," Dr. Patel laughed, referencing Bill Clinton as one of the presidential candidates in the 1992 election.

"I said QUENTIN," I retorted, patience worn thin by labor and not eating for an entire day. This made Dr. Patel laugh more, and though neither of us knew it at the time, I would be back to see him in less than five months, pregnant again.

I begged Craig to locate an apartment, but he was reluctant. His job was a new position, and he needed to show it was necessary. He worked long hours, and moving us into our own place was far from his mind.

It was never far from my mind. Living in close quarters with a baby who wouldn't sleep was almost more than I could bear. Every night I was up with Quentin, and every night as I rocked him, I would lament the loss of my own home, my own space, my autonomy outside motherhood.

Just when I had resigned myself to living with my in-laws indefinitely, Craig called me one day and asked, "How would you like to look at an apartment I've found?" After ten months of living out of boxes and bookshelves, we found our own place. Although Quentin still wasn't sleeping through the night (that would take another six months or so), I had my own space.

Our second son Morgan was born one year, one month, and one day after his older brother Quentin. I often said it was like having twins, though the older one could potentially hurt the younger, at least initially. The two boys grew up together, sharing clothes, toys, and a room, and while they were polar opposites in some of their interests, they shared a bond that grew to include their younger sister, born four years later.

Where is the Sting?

On the first day of class, Shari asked me if she could stand at the back of the classroom. "OK," I said with a quizzical look. "What's up?"

"I've got back problems. A couple of vertebrae that are going bad, pinched nerve, you name it." Her expression was placid, but I could see her jaw tighten as she shifted her weight from one leg to the other.

"Have you had this problem a while?"

She sighed deeply. "Yeah. I had a good job with health insurance and benefits, but now this back problem makes it impossible to do my job at the factory anymore." Shari leaned on the edge of my desk, using her elbow to prop herself up. "I have a daughter, too, who's counting on me. She's eleven and smart. She said she'll read over my papers for this class!"

We both laughed, and I asked her, "Do you have any other help?"

"My ex is no help at all. We were both big into drugs, then I got clean because of our daughter but he didn't. That was it—I had to get out. I have some help from my family," motioning to a younger woman sitting in a seat in the back row, "but they don't have a lot of money or time themselves."

Shari's niece Shannon, who was about fifteen years younger, sat in a seat near the back of the room. For the first major assignment, I typically had the class write a brief narrative about an incident that changed their lives. I was always amazed at what these students would freely tell me, the pen and paper acting as a cathartic for the wounds they suffered: loss, addiction, bad choices, even rape.

Shannon's narrative gripped me: she was sixteen-years-old when she was raped by a relative. When Shannon became pregnant from the rape and her son was born nine months later, she decided to keep him. "Everyone was telling me to give him up. My mom, my Aunt Shari, everybody. 'Put it all behind you,' they'd tell me. But I knew that two wrongs don't make a right, and if I gave him up, I'd have another wrong I'd be trying to forget," Shannon wrote. As I read her account, I was inspired by her courage and bigheartedness, yet I was ashamed that I might have chosen an easier path. I felt spoiled by my traditional, fairly functional upbringing—how did I get so lucky? It grieved me that decency and stability were so hard to come by in families these days.

She was about twenty-five when I met her, a lack of makeup and her freckles making her look younger. Shannon always had her assignments completed on time and her class attendance and participation were exemplary, evidence of the way the early experience of parenthood created a sobering sense of responsibility, I guessed. She cared for her nine-year-old son, working a couple of minimum wage jobs, as well as helping her disabled Aunt Shari care for her eleven-year-old daughter.

When our class discussion included the argument that the American welfare system needed reform, some students debated the need for welfare at all. "A lot of people just don't wanna work," one younger student offered, and others agreed, nodding their heads.

"So if you lose your job, and you have a family to take care of, how do you live until you find another job?" I asked.

"You move in with your folks and then go get another job," he countered. I could see some of the students, older ones who perhaps had experienced job loss and lack of financial security, getting agitated.

"But what if your folks are dead and you don't get along with your brothers or sisters? You got no family to help—what then?" said an older student named Paula. The younger student, who most likely had a traditional, functional family like me, was suitably chastised and appropriately silent. Paula went on, "I think it's a crock to say that people on welfare are lazy and don't want to work. The problem is that the jobs don't pay enough to support a family. And welfare doesn't cover everything when you're looking for a job."

A recipient of welfare aid, Shannon had an insider's view of what was wrong with the system. "It's so unfair all the hoops you have to jump through to get any help," she explained to the class. "I can get grants to go to school," Shannon shared, "but then I don't have the money for gas to get here. We don't have public transportation in rural areas, so it's like they don't think the whole process through."

Shannon's experience with welfare also made her well-acquainted with those who abuse the system. "One woman in my apartment complex has four kids, and she told me she wants to get pregnant with another so she can get more welfare money," Shannon said as she shook her head. "It's people like her that make it hard for people like me and my aunt to get help." Frustrations with the system drove Shannon to seek a degree in social services with plans to transfer to a four-year university to complete her bachelor's and advocate for change in welfare policies. I admired her passion and drive to create change that might help someone like her in the future.

Discussions like this one made my day. I loved how the more mature students like Shari, Shannon, and Paula could offer a depth of life experience to the younger students so they might see how their thinking only skimmed the surface bubbles, not plumbed the depths. Though I wasn't sure the younger students always listened, I knew that they were exposed to reality much more than I was as an undergrad at a typical four-year university.

One day I walked into our class, and I noticed Shannon sitting by herself. "Where's Shari today?" I asked as I passed back the graded writing exercises.

"She's got it really bad in her back today, and the pain meds they gave her make her so dizzy she can't walk very well," Shannon explained. "She's out in the car, and if you can come out and talk with her after class, she'd really appreciate it."

I followed Shannon out to her car after class and found Shari reclined in the front seat of an old Dodge, window rolled down. "Hi, Shari. What's going on?"

Shari tried to sit up but then eased herself back down again. "I'm sorry I had to miss class, Mrs. Kuhlman," she said. "I had a really bad spell last night with my back, and they gave me some different painkillers that really messed me up." Shari shook her head as if she were trying to clear it. "I know the rough draft of our problem-solving paper is due, and I've started it, but I was hoping you could see if I'm on the right track. It's here on this flash drive. Can you copy it?"

Her eyes looked pinched from the pain and the drugs, so I took the flash drive into my office and copied her document, then went back out to Shannon's car in the parking lot. "I'll look it over tonight and email you, Shari. You take care."

Shannon started her car, engine sputtering at first, and I could hear her muffler as she drove away. I went back to my office to look at what I had copied from Shari. Her argument was that the government needed to provide more assistance in the form of financial and academic support to older college students who were often either displaced or disabled factory workers. Though she started off strong, soon the paper became her personal testimony:

> Older students, especially those who are disabled, struggle to learn because of their age and the medication they are on. When they lose their jobs, their entire reality shifts. At that moment, all they know is they don't have another forty years to figure it out. Some have made mistakes; their bodies fail, and they blame themselves. It is hard for them to accept that this is not just another screw-up on their part, but a difficulty that needs to

be grieved to move through and forward. When they begin college, the advisors need to take these factors into account. Otherwise, the older students feel like they are going in circles, making choices based on survival instead of what will benefit them long-term.

The rest of her rough draft continued in this vein with few academic sources but plenty of life experiences to back up her points. Her dilemma with reality was a little similar to the dilemma I faced in critiquing her writing. I was torn between my responsibility to meet the standards of college-level research writing and my responsibility as a human being to encourage another person when she is down. I emailed her that evening:

Hi Shari,

I hope you're feeling a little better. I've looked through your draft and made some suggestions on the attached copy. I noticed that you have relied on your personal experiences rather than academic sources in this draft. While I think it is therapeutic for you to write about your experience, and while I hold these words gently in my heart with utmost compassion, you need to use outside sources for your evidence. Let me know if you need help locating good sources for this project.

The next week both Shari and Shannon were in class. "The doctor changed my meds, and I'm doing much better. He's planning to do surgery at the end of the semester, so I'm hoping that will take care of this pain." Shari went on, "I also found some really good sources, so I'll have a better rough draft for you later today."

She followed through on her promise, and her final draft made an impressive argument for the government to channel support toward retraining older, displaced, or disabled workers rather than paying them disability or allowing them to collect welfare. She managed to locate good sources that showed significant savings from retraining rather than sidelining these workers, and she substituted these academic sources for her personal experiences, making a solid academic argument. I was thrilled with her progress, but somehow found the academic argument less compelling and poignant than her swan song original draft despite the earlier draft's lack of adherence to the typical protocol for college-level academic writing.

I saw neither Shari nor Shannon over the summer term or in the fall, but I was only on campus two days a week so I was certain that I must have missed them. One gray January day I was in the copy center when Shannon came in. "How are you, Shannon? What are you doing these days?"

"I'm an office intern for the registrar, and I'll graduate with my associate's in May. I'm already accepted at

Bowling Green State University, and they've promised an academic scholarship — renewable. Can you believe it?"

"That's great news! I'm so proud of you and so happy to hear you're doing well."

Her smile froze for a second, and then went away. "You probably haven't heard about my Aunt Shari, have you?"

I shook my head.

"She had the back surgery, and while it helped her pain, afterward she started having heart problems. They said it was connected with her thyroid because she was losing her hair, gaining weight, and having other problems." She swallowed hard and took a deep breath. "The doctor had just set her up on thyroid medication. She had only been on it a few days when she had a massive heart attack out of the blue and died. This happened three weeks ago." Her eyes glistened with tears. "She was only forty-two years old."

I put my hand on her arm, stunned. "I can't believe it. I am so sorry for your loss, for her daughter's loss. Where's her daughter staying?"

"She's been staying with me mostly, but sometimes she stays with my mom. Her dad won't have anything to do with her since she chose Shari to live with after the divorce. Not that that's a big loss. He says he's not into drugs anymore, but I wouldn't believe him."

"I'm glad she's with you. You're the kind of role model Shari would want her girl being around."

Shannon squeezed my hand. "Thanks for everything," she said as she wiped her eyes with her fingertips, careful not to smudge her eye makeup.

I watched her leave as the copier clicked and hummed like a hospital ventilator, printing more writing exercises, which would mean more grading. *The never-ending stack of grading. Shari's short, pain-filled life. The brevity of life. Life goes on in spite of loss. Life must go on because of loss.*

I pulled my phone out of my purse and texted my husband: "Too tired to cook or grade tonight. Want to eat out and see a movie? xxoo."

Sitting Together

Mark came into my developmental writing class slowly the first day, using a cane to steady himself as he dragged his right leg behind him. His head wobbled a little as he talked, his speech a little slow and slurred. I wondered if he was a veteran who had sustained a brain injury, though I couldn't detect any visible scars. Maybe he was the victim of a stroke, but he didn't look much older than thirty.

We were working on thesis statements one day in class. The students gave me their thesis statements, and I wrote them on the whiteboard. My handwriting is atrocious, and if it is coupled with having to write on a vertical surface, it can be really difficult to read. I usually confess and apologize before I start just to get that off my chest, and students find it funny that an instructor will admit freely, even in a self-deprecating way, that she is not perfect.

"You should see my handwriting," Mark chortled, and I had noticed how slowly he wrote, painstakingly creating the letters as if they were Chinese calligraphy.

"See! I'm not the only one," I teased them. "Who else has lousy handwriting?" A number of other students raised their hands. "Well, thank goodness we type our major assignments!"

After the class dismissed, Mark stayed around for help with his thesis statement. Though I was curious about his medical condition, he was the one who brought it up, sharing that he had a progressive brain disease where his brain was literally shrinking. As one might suspect, this also shrunk his life expectancy, giving him maybe fifteen more years of life. Mark was thirty-four years old.

I asked him how he knew something was wrong, and he told me he used to be a truck driver. "One day I was dropping off a load at the local Walmart, and the guy in receiving said I was slurring my words. He thought I was drunk, and he turned me in. But I wasn't drunk. They ran tests, and they found out that I have this genetic disease," he said, shaking his head. "The chance of each parent carrying this defective gene is like one in a couple million, and both my parents are carriers. They had three kids: my sister, brother, and me. I'm the winner of the defective gene." His tone was sarcastic, but his eyes were starting to glisten as he went on.

"I mean, I have a wife and a nine-year-old daughter. I've always worked hard and tried to live right. Now I can't drive a truck anymore, so I'm retraining for a desk job. I need something to do until I can't work. I think, why me? Then there's my sister. She's the screw-up from hell. Drugs, one guy after another. Her life is a mess, but she's healthy; at least she is as healthy as a person can be when they do drugs, drink, smoke, and sleep around. Where's the fairness in that?"

"I don't know, Mark," I said, wishing that I had an answer and not knowing how to help. My typical tendency is to rush in and try to fix something in situations like this, whether it is emotional pain or physical pain, as compassion makes me empathize closely and I want to be rid of the felt pain almost as much as the person suffering does. This time, though, I had no way to help or fix, so I sat quietly and listened, holding his pain in my palms as he told me his story.

He expressed his concern for his daughter and cried over the time he would miss with her. I sat with Mark in the middle of his mess, and I shared a small piece of his suffering. After he finished, Mark told me he thought he understood the thesis statement enough to get started, though we really hadn't talked about that. He slowly got up to leave, the cane steadying him, and I began to pack up my things into my case.

I heard a thud at the back of the room, and I stood up to see that Mark had fallen at the back of the classroom. I ran to the back of the room. "Are you OK? Should I call someone for help?"

"I'm alright," Mark said as he used his cane to move a chair closer to him so he could pull himself up. "This happens to me all the time." Though I wanted to help him up, a part of me knew he needed to preserve his dignity, what little he had left. He managed to get into the chair, and from there, he stood up again and made his way out the door, leaning heavily on his cane.

As I watched him lumber down the hallway toward the parking lot, I thought about what the Zen masters say constitutes true enlightenment: those who are enlightened are not perfect; instead, they are not anxious about being imperfect. They say the point is not to perfect your life, your body, or your personality, but to perfect your ability to love that which is imperfect about yourself and others.[10] My conversation with Mark was part of his wrestling with imperfection, change, and death, and his struggles simply mirrored my own in an exaggerated way.

I saw Mark around campus over the next two years, and then I assumed he graduated. The last time I saw him was in the waiting room of a physical therapy clinic about five years after our class concluded. As I flipped through a magazine, I noticed a younger man using a walker make

---

[10] Kornfield, Jack. "Loving Kindness – Ep. 31." *Mindpod Network from Jack Kornfield*, 2 Oct. 2015, mindpodnetwork.com/jack-kornfield-ep-31-loving-kindness/.

his way into the room. His physical therapist happened to be at the desk, and he greeted him. "Well, Mark, what trouble have you gotten into since I saw you last week?"

Mark's speech was a little more slurred, his gait more awkward and stilted, but his sense of humor was still intact. "You don't wanna know, Dave," he kidded as the two of them walked back to the therapy room.

Sensory Images

Jared sat at the back of our classroom, right beside the door. This didn't seem odd to me at first because most students congregated at the back of the classroom, leaving the first row or two of seats empty. He was a Marine veteran of the Iraq War, a giant of a man with a full beard who always wore a cap. In fact, I only saw him take his cap off once, and it was then I noticed it: the long, white, waxy scar that started on his left temple and ended somewhere up in his hairline above his forehead. This was not his only scar; most were unseen—as evidenced by our class discussions.

"So let's think about what today's reading assignment reveals regarding how an author constructs an academic argument," I started off. We were discussing Aldous Huxley's essay "Propaganda Under a Dictatorship," noticing his comparison of Hitler's use of modern technology of his day, such as the radio and loudspeaker, to rally the people to his cause, with techniques of modern-day advertisers.[11] "Huxley points out that Hitler had a low opinion of people, believing that they were easily manipulated especially when in a crowd. And he found that an orator could more easily sway a crowd than if the people read the same speech printed out in a newspaper. Why is that?"

"I think it has something to do with 'herd-poison,'" an older student named James said.

"And what's 'herd-poison?'"

James flipped through his book to the Huxley essay, pages making a rasping sound, ears beginning to redden, so I pointed to another student. "Jules, can you define 'herd-poison?'"

Jules was already on the right page, and she said, "It's like a crowd gets caught up in the event or the energy of an event. If people were just reading by themselves, they might think differently about what was being said."

I nodded my head in agreement. "How many of you have ever participated in doing 'The Wave' at a sporting event? You know what I'm talking about: where a section of the stadium stands up and throws their arms in the air, and then the section beside, and the next, all the way

---

[11] Huxley, Aldous. "Propaganda Under a Dictatorship." *The Millennium Reader,* edited by Stuart Hirschberg and Terry Hirschberg, Pearson Education, Inc., 2009, pp. 261-266.

around the stadium. There's an old movie that shows how we can go along with the crowd without even thinking about it. Have any of you ever watched *When Harry Met Sally?*" A few hands went up, surprising me. "I want to play you a short clip where Harry and his friend are at a Giants game in the stands, and Harry is telling his friend about how his wife just left him."

Jared turned off the lights since he was by the door, and we watched the clip which showed Harry sharing painful details about his wife leaving him after asking for a divorce, but each time "The Wave" went around the stadium, both he and his friend stood up and threw their arms in the air.[12] Students started to giggle, catching the irony of the devastating news Harry was sharing while he was mindlessly participating in a crowd move.

"Does that illustrate the point about 'herd-poison'?" Heads nodded. "So if we think about how Hitler used the technology of his day, combined with our human tendency to follow a crowd, can anybody explain how today's advertisers and politicians use similar techniques, just more advanced technology?"

"Well, I think that advertisers appeal to people's basic needs, like wanting to be accepted or liked," one student offered. "Hitler knew the people wanted security, wanted jobs, so he played to their basic needs, too."

---

[12] Movieclips. "When Harry Met Sally... (4/11) Movie CLIP - Harry's Divorce (1989) HD." *Youtube.com,* 20 Mar. 2015, www.youtube.com/watch?v=MQRZuEppgT0.

"Politicians do the same thing, but they talk in such a way that they don't really say anything," another said.

The discussion continued with several students commenting, but ultimately Jared said, "I think George W. Bush took advantage of a herd mentality after 9/11 to get people to support the Iraq War." Jared's technique of somehow connecting our discussion topic back to the Iraq War reminded me of the joke about "the six degrees of Kevin Bacon," because he was always able to somehow weave the injustice of war into our discussions.

"I spent my first wedding anniversary in a bunker in Fallujah," he told the class one day. "Explosions, gunfire. I was scared out of my wits, and I wasn't sure I'd ever see my wife again." I watched as the other students listened, wanting to be respectful yet feeling a little uncomfortable, the way you might feel weird if you asked how someone's grandmother was and they told you she died last week. None of us knew the best or most helpful way to support him as he worked through his experiences in the Middle East.

After class, when everyone else had left, he came up to my desk. "Mrs. Kuhlman, I have to miss class next Tuesday because I have to go to court."

"OK." This wasn't the first time I had a student who missed class because of a court appearance, and I knew better than to ask for details. If they wanted me to know, they usually told me.

"I'm not in trouble or anything," Jared went on. "But I'm trying to prove I'm disabled so that I can get the veterans' benefits I'm entitled to. I've got PTSD, and I have to take medication to calm me down. Right now the military classifies me as seventy-five percent disabled, and I'm trying…"

Someone in the hallway dropped a bunch of books, creating a loud thud. Jared stopped talking, warily looking toward the hallway. When it was clear that everything was OK, he apologized, "Sorry about that. Loud noises tend to bother me." He took a deep breath. "Anyway, I'm trying to prove that I can't function without medication because of the Iraq War."

In an earlier narrative assignment, Jared shared about his role as part of the "clean-up" crew, a unit called to clean up an area, often in response to a roadside bomb explosion and occasionally, a suicide bomber. One time Jared and his unit were called after a suicide bomber blew himself up, and he described the carnage he witnessed: "Our job was to make an area look like nothing had happened, but that was a tough job when there were guts and blood all over the place and smoke that smelled like burnt hair. As we were cleaning up the site, one of the guys found the bomber's penis, still intact. He put it on a pole for a while, and we all had a good laugh about that." As I read about Jared's experience and his unit's response, I thought about the saying, "If I don't laugh, I'll cry," and I wondered how a person erases a memory with sounds and smells and images like that.

I saw Jared's picture in the newspaper a couple of years after our class concluded with his wife and four children, the oldest about eight-years-old and the youngest an infant. Habitat for Humanity was building a house for them, two stories with four bedrooms, two baths, and a basement, and in the picture, they looked so happy. The article said that the basement was intended for Jared to use if his PTSD flares up, giving him a quiet space away from the noise that four small children can generate. I pictured Jared there, using the dark quiet to calm what he must still see and hear and smell.

Learning at Home

While Craig was in college for his second bachelor's degree in theology, he had researched homeschooling as a viable educational option. A number of people we knew in Southern California homeschooled, mostly in response to the mounting school violence found in California's public system. Though we had landed back in Ohio, we still toyed with the idea of homeschooling our children.

With a lower cost of living, we were able to make it on one income, though it took a while to own a home. My days were filled with dirty hands and dirty bottoms, and while I loved staying home with our children, I longed for some intellectual pursuits. As our boys grew beyond toddlerhood, we started going to library storytimes and nature programs that the conservation club in our area promoted. These field trips gave me a taste of what homeschooling could be like. One program about the lowly groundhog, presented around Groundhog Day, looked interesting, and we were in need of an outing.

I loaded two little boys, ages three and four, into our gold Chrysler New Yorker, a hand-me-down from my father-in-law when he purchased a new car, and we headed over to the Johnny Appleseed Metropolitan Parks program. Since it was early in February, the program was called "Woodchucks, Groundhogs, and Whistle Pigs", and it was geared toward preschool children. The McElroy Environmental Education Center was nestled on the edge of one of the twelve park areas in Allen County, Ohio, which totaled over 1200 acres of woods. We registered at the door and settled in.

One of the park volunteers began taking around a stuffed groundhog, allowing the young attendees and their parents a close-up look at the teeth and claws. "Right now," the volunteer said, "groundhogs, who are also called woodchucks or whistle pigs, are just waking up from hibernating. Who knows what hibernating is?"

My oldest son's hand flew up. "It means they sleep all winter."

"That's right," the volunteer continued. "They sleep from October until spring, and they have litters of six pups or so in March or April."

The program continued, and my boys sat still, enraptured in learning about the hibernation habits of groundhogs. I watched them as they listened to the volunteer explain the intricate burrow system of groundhogs with its multiple entryways and exits. I wasn't going to test them on this; they were simply learning because they found the subject matter interesting.

As I sat back and observed them learning, I thought of the bodhisattva vow in Buddhism, where a person (or teacher) focuses on the truth of the work he or she is doing, and not on the hoped-for result of a new convert. Other related thoughts began to crowd my mind, such as the monk Thomas Merton affirming that a person seeking to awaken the world should not depend on any hope of a particular outcome.[13] By not placing expectations on our children, I would free them to learn without fear or judgment. Homeschooling would give me the freedom to do that, as I knew well how the public school system relied on rewards and punishments to make students conform. Maybe they wouldn't grow up to ace the SAT, but they would be interested learners. That was a goal that was worth sacrificing an income over.

On our way home from the park presentation, the boys excitedly chatted about groundhogs and what they learned that day. Their play with toy trucks and cars that day

---

[13] Kornfield, Jack. "Heart Wisdom: Emptiness, Creativity, and Joy" – Ep. 34." Mindpod Network from Jack Kornfield, 25 Sept. 2016, jackkornfield.com/heart-wisdom-ep-34-emptiness-creativity-and-joy/.

centered on watching out for groundhogs and creating groundhog burrows with their Lego blocks. I was a silent observer of their learning, listening to them decide who was going pretend to be the whistle pig first and how the toy box could be the place to hibernate for the winter, or at least until Mom called them for supper.

Chapter 5
Learning — Whose Responsibility?

Each One Different

Our oldest son Quentin could recite the days of the week, the months of the year, the letters of the alphabet, and his numbers from one to one hundred, with a minimum of errors. He was turning six at the end of August, and it was time to begin our homeschooling journey.

In preparation for the start of our homeschool, my husband and I attended a conference near our home to learn the state-mandated requirements of creating a private, non-chartered, non-tax-supported school in the state of Ohio. We listened to parents passionately defend their right to teach their children at home, a right that some had even endured jail time for back in the early 1980s. While we admired their devotion to strengthening the family bond, we noted that some of the attendees seemed a bit militant and fundamentalist in viewpoint, a sharp contrast to our personal beliefs.

"I like the idea of teaching our kids at home," my husband said, "but they aren't going to be weird and backward. We'll make sure of that."

At this conference, I met a retired schoolteacher who would evaluate current students (or new students like Quentin) and make curriculum recommendations. Because I had no clue what curriculum to use, we took him to see Mrs. Prudence Petty, who lived in a small town about an hour away. She had renovated an old garage, complete with air conditioning, where she housed her teaching books and met with students whom she evaluated or tutored. Mrs. Petty spent some time with Quentin in the pleasantly cluttered schoolroom/garage with its light green walls, allowing him to play with educational toys and quizzing him about some of the basics. After she completed her evaluation, she had my husband take Quentin outside to a swing set to play while she reviewed the results with me.

"Quentin is definitely ready for school," Mrs. Petty began. "He knows the typical basics required for kindergarten, as well as some extra things that most kids his age don't yet know or don't know very well." She went on to suggest certain books that I could order online, and when I was clear about how I should organize my school days with him, she smiled and said knowingly, "Quentin is going to be a lot of fun to school at home."

I had already enjoyed the preschool prep we had done together: lots of reading aloud, cutting with scissors, and coloring. Her words boosted my confidence that watching someone learn could be fun.

"Morgan, let's put together the ABC train puzzle," I said to my middle son on his first day of homeschool kindergarten. The ABC train puzzle was almost six feet long, with upper and lowercase letters on each "car" of the train, as well as a corresponding animal or item that matched the appropriate sound for that letter. I got him started on it, and then I went to get his one-year-old sister Chloe out of her highchair. Juggling a first grader and a kindergartener with a toddler just learning to walk could be a challenge, each one possessing a different temperament and level of ability. I washed Chloe's hands at the sink and looked toward the room where Morgan was just finishing up the train puzzle. He had been working for the past year or so at putting together the puzzle and was pretty adept at that; now would come the real test.

We sang the ABC song together as I pointed at the letters, and after we finished, I said, "Show me the letter B, Morgan." He quickly pointed out the B car on the train with the baseball bat. "Where's the A?" Morgan pointed to the first car loaded with apples. "How about R, Morgan?"

He pointed to the T car with its turtle in tow. "No, that's the letter T. Where's the R?" He tried another guess: the letter P. "Not that one. How about this?" I pointed to the letter R, and we make the rolling sound, r-r-r-r-r-r, with our mouths and tongues. If I were comparing him to his older brother, I would be in despair, but Mrs. Petty's evaluation of Morgan before we started calmed my fears.

"He's not like his brother. He's a different boy, so your methods will need to be different," she told me a few weeks before we began Morgan's kindergarten class. "He will pick up what he needs to in his own time. You just need to be patient and don't compare him to your other son."

Every school day we worked on the ABC train, and for weeks he would mix up R with P and T, and each time I showed him the right car, the one with the red raspberries in it, and we would say, "R-r-r-r-r-r." Some days we took dry, red raspberry jello powder in a cake pan, and with a wet finger, he would write an R. If he got it right, he could lick his finger, but if not, we would shake the pan until the red, sugary powder was smooth and try again.

One morning after a month or so of kindergarten, Morgan put together the ABC train while I washed up his sister's hands after breakfast. I sat with her on the steps leading into the room as he put the Z caboose in place, watching him concentrate, and then I asked, "Where's the T?"

"Right here," he pointed confidently to the T car with the turtle.

"And where's the P?" I asked.

"This one," he said, pointing to the P car with the green pears.

I took a breath and asked, "Where's the R?"

"R-r-r-r-r," he said as he traced the curves of the R and pretended to eat the red raspberries.

"Yes!" I picked him up and swung him around as his little sister chewed on the A for apple puzzle piece.

From the time she was eighteen months old, our daughter Chloe would climb into a kitchen chair, throw a stuffed animal on the table along with a large, wide-ruled writing pad, and say, "I practice my writing." Her writing at that time was a scrawl, perhaps an artistic scrawl, and while she didn't really like to color, she was very interested in letters and how to shape them with a variety of colored pencils and markers. Her older brothers, six and seven years old, would shake their heads, thinking she was crazy to do schoolwork when she had another four years of freedom.

By the time the boys were eight and nine, I began to read C.S. Lewis's *Chronicles of Narnia* aloud to them right after lunch. They enjoyed the descriptions of Aslan, the great lion, and the White Witch, and though we read for thirty minutes, it seemed too short. Their younger sister Chloe was only four and didn't always want to sit with us, so I didn't force her. She would move freely between the living room and her room, bringing toys and dolls out to play with, being with us but not really participating in the read-aloud. From what I could tell, it seemed as if she was playing in her own world, not listening at all to the story.

One day we were going to begin where Peter, Susan, Edmund, and Lucy were in great danger. It had been a cliffhanger of an ending the day before, and despite their protests to read more, I declined, knowing that a little suspense goes a long way to fuel interest. I was just as fascinated as they were about what was going to happen next, so the three of us piled on the couch right after lunch, a boy on each side of me.

As if by clockwork, Chloe began dragging out her Barbie doll head, a life-size mannequin with a full head of blond hair to comb and style, as well as various hair bows and barrettes. She sat on the floor a few feet away, began brushing Barbie's hair, and said, "Well, I wonder what's going to happen to those kids. It sure didn't look good for them yesterday when we left off."

She proceeded to methodically brush the oversized doll head's hair, as I looked at her, mouth agape, shocked that she had been listening intently the whole time. "Well, aren't you going to start?" she said to me impatiently. "We have to see what happens next."

"OK," I responded obediently, opening the book to the chapter where we left off. "The battle was all over a few minutes after their arrival. Most of the enemy had been killed in the first charge of Aslan and his companions, and when those who were still living saw that the Witch was dead they either gave themselves up or took to flight..."[14]

Who Failed?

"Emily, I've marked a number of grammar errors in your essay, and I've shown you how to correct them. Given your grade on this assignment, I will allow you to redo it within one week, but I urge you to seek out a tutor as you would benefit from more one-on-one attention," I wrote on her first essay. I usually could tell from the first essay which students would need a tutor to make it through the course, so I tried to de-stigmatize the idea of getting a tutor in class.

"A tutor simply helps you put your thoughts down in written form, and by practicing this regularly with personal attention, you may not even need a tutor for the last assignment or two," I told the class. "You shouldn't think that getting a tutor means you're stupid. I can tell you have the material down, but you need to practice

---

[14] Lewis. C.S. The Chronicles of Narnia: The Lion, the Witch, and the Wardrobe. Scholastic, Inc., 1950, p. 178.

putting it in written form. Having a tutor sit with you will also help with the frustration that comes with learning to write." I showed them a *YouTube* interview of author Ta-Nehesi Coates sharing how even after he revises his writing a number of times, he still only achieves about seventy-five percent of what he really has envisioned in his head.[15] They were interested in his interview, but I wasn't sure they were convinced.

Later in our class discussion, we talked about an excerpt by Mark Salzman called "Lessons" from his book *Iron and Silk*. In Salzman's memoir, he taught English to a Chinese expert in martial arts in exchange for martial arts lessons. His Chinese instructor (whose name was Pan) told him that if a student fails or performs badly, it reflected poorly on his teacher as if the student had not been properly taught. One evening Pan had Salzman and a few of his friends over for dinner when he decided to recite some of the English sentences he had been learning. Pan concentrated fiercely and became very focused as he quickly recited the sentences eight times over without stopping. When Salzman congratulated him for his fine effort, Pan told his guests, "I was very nervous just then. I didn't want him [Mark Salzman] to lose face."[16] The students in my class found it novel that the Chinese

---

[15] The Atlantic. "Creative Breakthroughs: Ta-Nehisi Coates." *YouTube*, 27 Sept. 2013, youtube.com/watch?v=6voLZDYgPzY.

[16] Salzman, Mark. "Lessons." *The Millennium Reader*, edited by Stuart Hirschberg and Terry Hirschberg, Pearson Education, Inc., 2009, pp. 213-218.

cultural tradition allows that failure on the part of the student creates a loss of face for the teacher.

This cultural revelation spurred a student named Joyce to blurt out, "Some teachers could care less if their students learn anything. My art history instructor told us we weren't even allowed to ask questions. What's up with that?"

Others concurred that some instructors are intimidating and difficult to approach. "They seem like they are out to get you," Katelyn said, "like they want you to fail."

This led into more discussion about whose responsibility it is to learn, and whether failure should be split 50/50 between teacher and student, or if there are situations when a student (or a teacher) has not put forth adequate effort, thus skewing that equitable split. I managed to lasso the discussion somehow and tied it back to the need to pay attention to feedback and utilize a tutor.

Emily was one of the students who needed a tutor, and though I gave her a chance to revise/redo, she didn't hand a revision in one week later. That same day, I was in the Writing Lab, an open lab where all students at the college can show up for writing help on a first-come, first-served basis, and Emily came in to see me.

"Mrs. Kuhlman, I had no idea that my writing was bad. I was so shocked when I got my paper back and saw the grade," she shook her head in disbelief. "When I was in high school, my English teacher would only mark one or two things and then give me a B."

This wasn't the first time that I had heard of students being moved through the public school system without learning the basics. In another class, I had a student who confessed that he never learned to read until ninth grade when a high school teacher noticed and spent extra time helping him. He was a bright young man, though I suspected he was unruly, and with his late advent into the world of reading, his spelling was not the best. I sympathized with students who were pushed through the system because of state-imposed teaching to the test or because they were discipline problems that no one wanted to deal with.

"Why didn't you redo the assignment and turn it in on time like we discussed?" I asked, still not completely convinced of her sincerity.

"I work full-time at the grocery store, and we've been short-handed due to one head cashier being on leave due to a serious illness," she said, mouthing the word "cancer" as if it were too terrible to speak. "I wanted to ask if I could have until this weekend to redo it."

My typical policy on assignments allowed a student to redo the assignment, subject to a late penalty, if the revision was turned in one week after receipt of the graded copy. I hesitated. Something seemed off. "Why didn't you email me about your time crunch?"

She looked down and I thought I saw her eyes tear up. "I've just been so busy; I didn't even think of it."

"OK," I told her. "You can have until this weekend to complete it. But you really need to get a tutor. Have you looked into that yet?"

She assured me she would have it emailed by the weekend, though she hadn't had a chance to get a tutor. Yes, she would definitely look into that.

The weekend came and went, and our Monday morning class rolled around. No email from Emily, and she missed class, too. The next writing assignment was due on Wednesday. Later that day she showed up in the writing lab again.

"Mrs. Kuhlman, I'm so sorry I didn't get the revision emailed to you this past weekend. I had to cover two shifts, and I ran out of time. I wanted to let you know that I'm taking two weeks' vacation starting today to get myself caught up. I'll have the revision to you by email tonight. Could you help me by looking through what I have for the next assignment due Wednesday?"

Against my better judgment, I agreed, and we worked through the hodge-podge of material she had thrown together for the next assignment. Later that evening, her emailed revision of the first assignment appeared, but it was only slightly revised from the original. She had clearly not used a tutor to help, nor did she pay attention to the feedback I provided on the graded essay. I was beginning to feel like I was in the movie *Groundhog Day* again, re-grading the same material over and over.

Her subsequent assignments followed suit, and when her rough draft of her largest research assignment revealed she had plagiarized about sixty-five percent of it from her sources, she finally decided she should get a tutor. But "a tutor used late does not good writing make" — a maxim about writing that Emily learned later rather than sooner. She didn't make it through the class, and I realized I had been well-played by a student who had no desire to improve.

I saw her in the grocery store after that semester ended. She noticed me but then acted busy, adjusting the racks of gum or asking other customers if they needed help finding anything. I pretended I was busy, too, scanning my groceries at the self-check lane. I reflected on Salzman's experience with Pan, realizing this must be how "losing face" feels for both of us.

Right but Wrong

It set me off a little that he was on *Facebook* in class instead of working on his writing assignment like everyone else. This probably was partly because it was my first semester teaching at the college, and at that time, my expectations for student attentiveness were much higher than they were once I had more teaching experience. Because my instructor computer allowed me to view what each student was working on and even project that on the smartboard screen, I had an idea to combat students' lack of attention.

"Everyone should be finishing their journal entry for today, not looking at *Facebook*," I said in my most authoritative tone. Some students looked up and started to giggle, and once the laughter started, James finally looked up and saw his smiling *Facebook* profile picture looking back at him from the smartboard. His face darkened with a scowl as he closed out the page, and while I felt a certain sense of satisfaction knowing that James and the rest of the class would be less likely to venture into social media during class time, I had a vague sense that one-upping him might not have been the best idea.

Still, I had confessed that this was my first semester teaching at the college, and I had hoped for a little patience as I worked out best practices in the classroom. Though I knew grammar and writing basics, I had to figure out how to make them make sense to students who had no affinity for words. I thought by being honest about my lack of experience in the classroom, students would remember the Golden Rule and show me the compassion they would like to receive if they were in my position. Most were gracious; James was not.

As I was grading daily journal entries at home one day after class a number of weeks into the semester, I noticed that I didn't have a journal entry for James even though he had been in class that day. I remembered him working on the computer, though I hadn't verified that he was typing the journal entry. *Rats! He probably is trying to put one over on me again,* I thought as I cleaned out my school bag just in case his journal was misfiled. After I couldn't find a journal writing for James, I decided that this would require another moment of "tough love," allowing him to experience the consequence of not submitting a journal entry by earning a zero out of five points for the assignment. The journal only represented one-half of a percent of his total score, and since this was a developmental course, he only needed to earn a seventy-five percent to pass the class. *This will be a good lesson for him,* I thought as I considered how he disregarded my feedback on assignments, continuing to make the same mistakes over and over.

Ever since I projected his computer screen with his *Facebook* profile picture on the class smartboard, James and I had been at odds. He often challenged me in class discussions over the slightest point, and I felt I needed to prove myself right through extra explanations, so shaky was my teaching presence, and I used up extra class time I had originally planned to spend with those who were really struggling. I began to question the wisdom of being "right" when I embarrassed him that day in class.

The next class I passed back the graded journals, and James did not receive one. "Hey, where's mine?" he questioned as I walked to the front of the class.

"I didn't have a journal in my stack for you," I told him. "It looks like you didn't complete one."

"But I did!" he insisted, looking around at his classmates for support. The rest of the class began to look uncomfortable as if they were voyeurs of a domestic squabble.

"I'm sorry, James," I said as I took out the handouts for that day's lesson. "I can only grade what I have in front of me. It's only five points, and I'm sure you'll be certain to turn in the rest of them."

"But I did it, I know I did it!" His reaction to misplacing a five-point assignment was out-of-proportion to the impact those points would have on his overall grade. James began to talk under his breath, muttering. I couldn't make it out, and I was sure that was for the best.

As I started that day's lesson, he abruptly picked up his backpack and walked out. Part of me was relieved; his classroom presence and demeanor seemed to agitate the class and me. Without him there, I was able to get through the planned lesson and spend some extra time with struggling students, but I felt a nagging sense that I didn't have the whole story. I wasn't sure I really wanted to know the whole story.

James missed the next class. And the next one, too. We had a major writing assignment coming up worth one hundred points, and I wasn't sure if he was going to be prepared. As I walked through the atrium where students hung out, ate, and studied, I saw James sitting at a table by himself. He was working on homework for another class, but I decided to interrupt him and find out what was going on.

"Hi, James." I smiled and sat down across from him. "How have you been? I haven't seen you in class for a while."

"I'm alright. Just trying to get my drafting homework done." He barely looked up from his book, but I noticed he looked tired, and he lacked that spark that he typically brought to class, the very one he often used to challenge me.

Determined to find out what was going on, I said, "What's going on with you, James? You fought with me over a five-point assignment that I never received, but it looks like you're willing to forego a one-hundred point assignment that will actually impact your chances of making it through this class. I don't get it."

James pushed the drafting book aside, leaned back in his chair, and took a deep breath. "I don't know. I'm in over my head. This is my first semester in college, and I've got eighteen credit hours—six classes. On top of that, I work thirty hours or more a week for a farmer who lives nearby. I thought I could handle it, but I can't. I won't be coming any more to your class because I'm trying to make it through these other classes, and something had to give." He shook his head and looked down at his hands, callused and rough from farm labor. Defeated.

It was past the date to withdraw with a "W" from classes, so I knew that wasn't an option. Despite our differences, I felt bad that he was learning his limitations in such a way that would impact his GPA and his financial aid. "Look, I'll help you with the one-hundred point essay, and if you can't make it to class, you can submit assignments through email. You only have about a month or so to go."

He shook his head again. "No. I'm done. I'm not even sure that I want to go to college anymore. Thanks anyway." He picked up his drafting book again and started on his homework. Our conversation was finished.

"Good luck, James," I said as I picked up my bag, wishing I had thought about the rule "Do unto others what you would have them do to you" when I had projected his *Facebook* picture on the classroom smartboard and feeling sorry that I was part of the bad taste in his mouth from his college experience.

I'll Make It

My husband advocated for our children working as soon as they were old enough, believing that the responsibility could teach them important lessons that would serve them well as adults. "I had a paper route when I was just ten years old," he told me. "In fact, I had the biggest *Toledo Blade* Sunday paper route in the city of Findlay."

"Didn't your dad have to drive you every Sunday morning because you had too many papers to carry on your bike?" I asked, recalling my father-in-law's distaste for the paper route. I knew that a paper route would end up being my job, at least in a supervisory capacity, and though I was far from thrilled, I agreed that the larger life lessons might be worth it.

The boys began a paper route at the ages of eleven and twelve. Though they didn't like having to get up at 5:00 in the morning to have the route delivered by 7:30, they really liked having their own money. They especially liked Christmas time when the gifts and tips from their subscribers began to roll in, adding up to $675 one year. Occasionally, subscribers (mostly older senior citizens) would include a thank you note, and one included a $5 tip for "the paper boys' mother." I was now an official paper carrier.

Once Quentin hit the age of sixteen, he picked up a job pushing carts for a local grocery store. This meant the paper route would belong to his younger brother and their sister, who had seen her brothers' paychecks and Christmas tips and was ready to make her own money. Chloe was eleven, so I knew I had five more years of newspaper delivery to look forward to.

At the same time he started working at the grocery store, Quentin also began going to driver's education to qualify for his driver's license. For a few weeks, his schedule was busy: homeschool, working at the store, and then attending driver's training for four more hours in the evening. His spot at the family dinner table looked empty, and I knew that our family was moving into a new phase of life, one where sitting down together to share supper would be less of a practice. I worried about his hectic schedule since our homeschool atmosphere was more laidback, and I hoped that the pressure wouldn't be too much.

Craig and I were scheduled to go away on a business trip for three days, and the kids convinced us that they could fend for themselves without an official babysitter. Though neighbors were going to keep an eye on them, we hadn't yet figured out how Quentin would get to work. "I'll just take my driver's test before you leave," he told us. "I'll have all my driver's ed classes and all my supervised driving time done, so we can make an appointment. I'll have my license before you leave."

I was a little skeptical. We had been practicing the maneuverability part of the driving test in a store parking lot. It required moving the vehicle through cones without knocking any of them over, and during our practice time, a few cones had been upset. "We need a Plan B, just in case," I told him. "Maybe Kevin's mother could drive you. She's not working now, right?"

Quentin fixed his blue eyes on mine. "I'll pass it," he said with quiet confidence.

His demeanor and tone reminded me of the scene from the movie *Hoosiers* where the coach (played by Gene Hackman) tells the team to use a final play that doesn't include their star shot in an effort to throw the other team off.[17] In the movie, the team doesn't say anything, but their body language conveys their disagreement. Coach asks them what's wrong, and none of them want to challenge his decision, but the star shot Jimmy Chitwood simply says quietly, "I'll make it." The coach defers to him, and they win the game.

Quentin's confidence in spite of the pressure of a hectic schedule plus a driver's test amazed me. Though I hopefully didn't convey it, I was less confident. We had been unable to find anyone who could take him to work, there was no public transportation in rural northwestern Ohio, and it was too far to walk. His driver's test was scheduled for a Tuesday morning, and Craig and I were leaving on Thursday. If he didn't pass it, I would have to figure out a solution in one day. *He must have inherited his father's optimism*, I thought to myself. I preferred realism and planning for the worst. If the worst did not happen, it was all good, and if it did happen, well, I was ready with Plan B. Except I wasn't ready with a Plan B this time.

We showed up at the Bureau of Motor Vehicles, and I sat in the waiting area. Other parents crowded around the window which had a view of the maneuverability lot, but I couldn't watch. My stomach was in knots as I reviewed potential rides for Plan B. I was startled out of my thoughts by the sound of Quentin's voice.

---

[17] "HOOSIERS - State Championship game closing scenes." *YouTube*, uploaded by MrGeorgeE3, 13 Feb. 2011, www.youtube.com/watch?v=Y7YeUUoY90M.

"Hey, Mom, come on." He motioned me to go into the foyer outside the testing station. I planned my words carefully: *It's OK, honey. Lots of kids don't get their license on the first try. We'll figure out some way to get you to work while Dad and I are out of town.* I moved toward the door he propped open for me, but before I could say anything, he motioned me toward the licensing division across the hall.

"Come on. Maybe we can beat the line," Quentin urged me toward the office.

"So, you passed?" I asked incredulously.

He laughed. "Of course I passed. I told you I would." With that, he grabbed a number and took a seat to wait his turn.

He told me he would pass, I mused, *and he did.* Quentin's reservoir of self-confidence was full, and he moved forward, not needing a Plan B or preparing for the worst. Maybe I needed to say "I'll make it" more often and do less planning for the worst.

Chapter 6
Moving Forward Despite Our Wounds

More Than Just Mom

Following the advice of the community college president at my husband's economic forecast seminar, I mailed my resumé and cover letter to the dean. As I looked it over for the hundredth time before sending it, I shook my head. No teaching experience except teaching kindergarten through tenth grade, and this was not in a traditional school setting. It was a homeschool where the students (all three of them) often sat around doing math in their pajamas, and fixing dinner was included as part of a Life Skills class. I wasn't even sure what the word "pedagogy" meant, so I had to look it up. Not just once, but two or three times. Finally, I defined it as "a teaching method," and I was able to remember it, though I still felt as if my "pajamas pedagogy" was expected to be more academic than it was.

My background was in journalism, but the only outside work I had was freelance writing, mostly for a publisher of two local magazines, perhaps one or two articles per month for the past four years. For me, it was fun, a creative distraction when I was worn out from full-time mothering and schooling. My resumé revealed that I had not worked a full-time job in sixteen years and that my previous full-time job was as an insurance underwriter. *Ouch.* Other than my freelance writing, I had no professional writing experience, and other than homeschooling my own children, I had no professional teaching experience. *Double ouch.* I quickly put the letter and resumé in the smooth, linen-textured envelope, sealing it and walking out to the mailbox before I had a chance to talk myself out of sending it.

I dutifully called a week later to talk to the dean. She said she wouldn't need anyone until the fall schedule, which she hoped to be working on by April and that she would be in touch. March and April flew by, and though I called and left a message for her, I heard nothing.

My oldest son Quentin, almost a junior in high school, wanted to take college classes for dual credit at this community college, so I went with him to take the placement test in May. We drove on rural country roads edged with soybean fields that seemed to go on for miles. The level topography would have been good evidence for the ancient belief that the earth is flat, and the blue spring sky seemed close enough to touch. *Hard to believe this area was once a black swamp,* I thought as I pulled into the parking lot. The spaciousness of the fields was a sign of new life, springtime, and maybe something more.

After locating the testing center for my son, I settled down with a cup of tea from the small café to stare at the cornfield across the parking lot. The corn stalks were just babies, but I knew the saying, "Knee-high by the Fourth of July," promising the fast growth that would come followed by the harvest in September. *Much like the growth of our children*, I mused, thinking how not that long ago I had been working with them to learn their ABCs; now we struggled together through chemistry. I finished my tea and my reminiscing and then decided on the spur of the moment to stop in person to say hello to the dean. After asking for help, I located her office. She was pleasant, though a little surprised to see me.

"It's a pleasure to meet you, Dr. Smith. I've been a writer for years, and I'm really interested in teaching," I told her, trying not to sound nervous or talk too fast. *Keep it casual, Nan.* "How's the fall schedule coming along?"

She picked up a large folder, bulging with resumés and cover letters, and after some digging, she located mine. "Well, I'm still working on it," she said as she quickly read over my brief resumé. "I'm hoping to finish by the beginning of June." Given the stack of resumés in that folder, I could see she had a lot of work to do, and it was clear that meeting deadlines, even those self-imposed, was a challenge. I thanked her and left, feeling like I showed up to a party I wasn't invited to.

Though my son passed his college placement test and was going to be able to take college-level courses for free through a state program, my happiness for him was tinged around the edges with disappointment over my meeting with Dr. Smith. *What was I thinking?* I berated myself. *It probably seemed pretty presumptuous to apply for a college instructor position without having a master's degree. I should have never gotten my hopes up.* Hope and disappointment struggled in my mind; disappointment and despair were winning this epic battle as I resigned myself to waiting to apply for instructor positions until I had finished a master's degree.

The phone rang on June 30. "Hello, is this Nanette Kuhlman? This is Terry Smith from Ohio Community College. Would you be available to teach one or two developmental writing courses this fall?"

I kept my composure, accepting two basic composition courses, but once off the phone, I ran around the house shrieking with glee, our three dogs yapping at my heels like I was a rabbit on the loose in the backyard. They clearly were not prepared for my ecstatic response, even as I began to feel unprepared for what I had committed to.

What about my pedagogy? The doubts started to come in like junk mail, telling me that my pajamas pedagogy would never be good enough. Yet it was all I knew. Despite the difference in ages between my homeschooled students and my college students, my method, I decided, would be the same: love them, encourage them, and still require them to do the work. Maybe the way I taught at home and the way I taught at the college would not be so different.

The disappointment I had felt when I thought I'd been passed by for this teaching opportunity was defeated for the time being, but like any worthy adversary, it would be back. And I would be ready.

The Strength of Elephants

Because I was going on a trip, I decided to splurge on a gel shellac for my nails. It was a Saturday when I called one of the local salons, and after I made the appointment for the following Monday, I received a text reminder: "You have an appointment at 10:00 Monday, Sept. 14 with Yolanda Rodriguez." *Yolanda Rodriguez*, I thought to myself. The name was familiar, and I could somewhat visualize her face, so I looked through my old grade books to see if she had been a former student. After some digging, I located her class. She had been in my beginning composition class two years before, and I remembered that her mother died when she was young, leaving her father and extended family to raise her.

The narrative she wrote for me about losing her mother was powerful. "I felt like I lost part of myself when she died," Yolanda wrote. "For a long time, I didn't want to live because I didn't know how to live without her. My dad saw I was having trouble, so he made an appointment to see a grief counselor. It was then that I knew I needed to live, not because I wanted to, but because my mother would have wanted me to." Her poignant narrative made plain the wisdom of letting others help with the grieving process.

The beauty salon was busy on a Monday morning, but Yolanda was at the reception desk to greet me. Her dark hair had interesting blue streaks through it, and it was cut into a flattering chin-length bob. She wore an off-the-shoulder asymmetrical top that revealed a large tattoo on the top part of her left arm. There were words and pictures, but I couldn't make them out.

Yolanda smiled and greeted me, "Hi, Mrs. Kuhlman."

"Hi, Yolanda. I wondered when I set up the appointment if it was you. How have you been?"

We walked back to her table surrounded by lots of colored polishes. "I've been fine. I'm still going to school. Nights mostly, now that I'm working on my bachelor's from Miami University. I work here all day Mondays and Wednesdays, and then I have class in the evening."

I knew that Miami University was a private school located a few hours away, so I figured it must be a satellite program. "Where do you go for classes?"

"I still go to Ohio Community College." She began to soak my right hand as she filed the left. "They have a special deal where I pay the community college rate per credit hour for the first ten classes before it bumps up to the higher rate."

"What are you studying?" I asked.

"Electrical engineering," Yolanda replied as she moved my left hand into the soapy water and started trimming the cuticle on the right hand. "I was raised by my dad, and he worked on cars, so I like the idea of working on the electrical system of cars."

"Wow, you are probably the only woman in the class, aren't you?"

Yolanda laughed. "There's one other girl in the class besides me, but it's OK. I can hold my own with those guys. My dad taught me how."

I noticed a beautiful engagement ring on her finger. "So you're engaged now?"

"Yes," she said, touching up the color on my left pinkie. "When I was in your class, I was engaged to someone else. That didn't work out; it wasn't good. My current fiancé was an old friend, someone I had known and worked with at another job. I had no idea that he liked me until I broke off my other engagement, and he called me to see if I wanted to hang out. He is a little older than me, but he's settled and has a good job. Treats me like a queen."

We continued to chitchat about school and life as she worked on my nails. I was trying to read the tattoo without much success, so I finally just asked. "Yolanda, I notice you have a tattoo with some words on your arm. What does it say?"

She turned her left shoulder toward me so I could read it. It was a Bible verse, I Corinthians 16:13-14: "Be on the alert, stand firm in the faith, act like men, be strong. Let all that you do be done in love." Below the tattoo was an elephant that reminded me a little of the Hindu god Ganesh that I had seen in some Indian art.

"So what's the significance of this verse for you?" I asked as she put the final coat of shellac on my nails.

"It is just my favorite verse," she said, "and since my dad raised me, I decided that I wanted to be strong and act like him. He was tough and firm but always loving. That's how I want to be."

"And what about the elephant?"

"My dad's mother, my grandmother, also helped take care of me, and she always liked elephants. When she passed away, I got this elephant to remember her." With that, Yolanda finished my manicure with a hand massage that had to be enjoyed in silence.

I paid her and thanked her for doing my nails, and as I drove home, I thought about a *National Geographic* video I watched which illustrated how elephants never forget. The video showed a young elephant, taken from her mother around age three and put to work for four years in the tourist industry before being reunited with her mother. The two appeared to remember each other, nuzzling and stroking each other.[18] Yolanda's tattoo encouraging her to

[18] Howard, Brian Clark. "Watch Touching Reunion of Rescued Elephant and Her Mother." National Geographic, 9 Apr. 2015,

be strong and to stand firm, illustrated with an elephant, seemed appropriate, and the pairing of her masculine father's influence with her grandmother's femininity seemed to have worked its way into her.

For a while, I puzzled about her choice of Bible translation for the verse since other translations did not include the phrase "act like men." Yet this is what she grew up with: a solid, strong, masculine presence. Yolanda's father gave her permission to be more than her gender typically allows in American culture, and her grandmother seemed to offer the feminine influence that young girls need. Her choice of this Bible verse appeared to acknowledge her ability to be strong in a man's world. Yolanda was going to be OK, even without a typical two-parent upbringing. As her favorite verse confirmed, all should be done in love, and love is a river that can have many tributaries and outlets.

Beat You to It

"I'm so sorry, Mrs. Kuhlman," Larry began. "I intended to get with a tutor this week, but it just didn't happen."

---

news.nationalgeographic.com/2015/04/150409-elephant-reunion-video-thailand-me-bai-behavior-science/.

"Sorry" was Larry's favorite word, the kind of word that was supposed to make palatable whatever was coming after it, sort of like a spoonful of sugar before the medicine. He used it frequently and freely, apologizing for oversights that may have been more an indication of laziness than actual forgetfulness. "Sorry" flew out of Larry's mouth almost as fast as the funny stories and offhand comments full of self-deprecating humor.

One time as I explained how to organize a causal analysis essay, I used the example of obesity, offering three ideas about possible causes. "Are you looking at me?" Larry interrupted my explanation. "I think she's looking at me," he wryly suggested to his nearby classmates.

"No, I wasn't looking at anyone in particular, Larry," I stammered, flustered and out-of-sync with my thoughts about causal analysis. "I was just using this as an example to help everyone understand how to set up their paper."

"It's OK," he grinned. "I know I'm fat. We were swimming in the river this past weekend, and my buddy said, 'Hey, Larry, here's a lifejacket.' And I said, 'Hey man, I don't need no lifejacket. I'm fat so I float!'" He stretched his arms out and laid his head back as if in a back float position.

Larry's classmates squirmed, unsure if they should laugh or feel sorry for him. I continued my explanation about causal analysis, wondering about the cause of Larry's behavior. He told me early in the semester that this was his second attempt at beginning composition, and that if he didn't pass, he would lose his financial aid and opportunity to go to college.

This time around, Larry had been placed in a Writing Workshop, a co-requisite, developmental class to help students improve their writing skills, hopefully increasing their chances of being successful in Composition I. Though he was often late showing up to Composition I, he almost always was early for the workshop class afterward. As I approached our classroom, I could hear him, entertaining his classmates with stories, his voice taking on a Southern drawl whenever it fit.

"My mama watches my little niece, and even though she's only three, she's obsessed with bras," he said to a couple of giggling female students waiting for the workshop to begin. "I called my mom the other day, and my niece got on the phone to tell me, 'I want boobies, so I can wear bras.'" Twitters of laughter from his listeners spiraled out into the hallway where I listened and graded papers.

"'Now Monica,' I tell my niece, 'you're jest a little girl, and little girls don't have boobies.' Next thing ya know, she starts to cry, bawlin' her head off, and my mom gets on the phone and says, 'Larry, what in the world did you say to her?' 'Mom, I only told her the truth—little girls don't have boobies.' My mom acts all pissed off, and says, 'Larry, next time keep yer truth to yerself.'" Larry's drawl increased each time he reiterated what his mother told him, and his female listeners responded with gales of laughter.

Larry's charm was apparent, and his knack for storytelling made up for his eccentricities among his classmates. Despite his admitted struggles with his weight, I always saw him with a crowd of young women, and from what I noticed, he was charming them with his wit and deference. Though he was always respectful toward me, saying, "Yes, ma'am," whenever I called on him, I sometimes sensed that Larry understood the usefulness of showing respect to those with authority over him. I easily imagined him trying to sell me an old Ford with a dangling tailpipe and being successful at it.

I suspected his charm was the result of the health issues he had suffered as a young child. Born with problems in the growth plates in his legs, he endured as many as twenty surgeries before he was a teenager. Even with the surgeries, Larry still walked slowly with a slight limp, dragging his left foot behind him. The multitude of surgeries affected him in other ways. "I've been told that having lots of surgeries when you're young makes you a little immature," he told me one time.

"How old are you, Larry?" I asked.

"I'm thirty-seven," he said, "but most people peg me around twenty."

I nodded my head in agreement. Larry looked younger than thirty-seven, and his lack of focus had all the marks of a teenager. As we were waiting for documents at the printer, an error message appeared: out of paper. I grabbed another ream out of the desk drawer, awkwardly tearing the wrapper piece by piece in my effort to remove it.

"Mrs. Kuhlman, now don't be scared," Larry said as he pulled something out of his pocket. It was a knife, and he clicked the switch to reveal a blade about six inches long. He took the ream of paper from me that I had been struggling to open, neatly slit the end of it, and then loaded the paper in the printer drawer. Strangely, the thought of being in danger never crossed my mind.

"I wanted to warn you so you wouldn't think I was going to misuse my knife," he said. "Some instructors would freak out over something like that. I think people have gone overboard with this whole ban on pocket knives and concealed carry guns."

Larry was an avid hunter, a card-carrying NRA member, yet for all his bravado, he surprised me with his reverence for animals. "Sorry my essay was a little shorter than the assignment called for," he began, "but I got a call from my buddy who lives in town. Seems he had a raccoon that was prowling around his property, and he finally caught him in a live trap. Problem was that he couldn't kill it in town, and the raccoon was acting so wild in the cage, he was scared to try to take it out to the country and let it loose. So he called me, and I picked up the raccoon to take him back to my place. That coon was a young one."

"Oh, you live in the country, and you were going to let it loose for him?" I questioned.

"No, I was going to kill it," Larry continued calmly. "But it was gettin' dark out, and I couldn't see real good. On my first shot, I didn't kill it. The little guy took his tiny black hands and covered his head, and he seemed so human-like, I almost couldn't finish the job." Larry shook his head. "You know, I'm part Native American, and Native Americans would thank the animal they killed for the food they would receive from it. They had quite a ritual built around the hunt for food."

I had also heard about Native Americans expressing gratitude toward the animals who provided food by giving their lives. I nodded my head in agreement, and before I could say anything, Larry had launched into another story, attempting to amuse the rest of the class and me.

"So one time we were on vacation in Key West, and I wanted to go parasailing," Larry started off. "My dad said he would take me, so we had to drive to another of the keys (I can't remember which one), and we went into the parasail place to sign up. The owner of that place took one look at me and said, 'Son, you might have a time gettin' airborne. I can't guarantee that we'll be able to get you up.' And I said, 'Sir, it sounds like you are calling me a fatty,' and his jaw practically hit the floor."

The room went silent, and we all looked at one another awkwardly, Larry's humor putting us all in that difficult spot where to deny the truth of what was said would be a lie. Just as I was going to change the subject to our workshop lesson, another student named Kayla said, "If you call yourself 'fat' one more time, I'm going to smack you."

Everyone in the class nodded, and I thought *Amen, Sister*, before I launched into our discussion for the day. Larry seemed unaffected by her comment, so ingrained was his tendency to point out his own flaws before someone else could make fun of him for it.

"Sorry if I talked too much today," Larry said after class. "I just think of these funny stories, and I like to make people laugh. I really shouldn't talk so much."

Though I knew I was being manipulated into saying it, I willingly said, "It's OK, Larry. Your storytelling is a gift, one that will probably serve you well someday." He looked at me a little incredulously, mumbled his thanks, and limped down the hall. I watched for a while, reminded of the little raccoon covering his head with his black hands, trying to protect himself the only way he could.

Quirks and Connection

I had agreed to teach four composition classes, two beginner and two advanced, this term. What I hadn't agreed to was the overloaded classes: each one had at least twenty-five to thirty-one students when a full class was considered to be twenty-four students and no extra compensation was given for teaching extra students.

Charlie was in one of the advanced composition classes, and from the first day, I knew he would be a challenge. He was extremely articulate with a wide vocabulary, and anytime I asked the class a question, he was first with his hand in the air. In fact, if I called on him first he was quick to monopolize the entire class discussion. He was the youngest child in his family, he said, with an older brother who was a medical doctor (and an asshole, in his opinion), and he shared in class about his attention-deficit disorder and Tourette syndrome. On our first day together, he greeted me with a fist-bump in class. I was stretched beyond what I thought I could handle work-wise, and I had Charlie.

Our first short story discussion was about "The Oblong Box" by Edgar Allan Poe.[19] Many of the students were familiar with Poe's work, having already read "The Raven" or "The Tell-Tale Heart," so encouraging them to read Poe was an easy task. "The Oblong Box" was one of Poe's more obscure works, but it had the typical suspense-building quality they loved. The story of the narrator's college friend who brings an oblong pine box, tightly sealed, on a sea journey from South Carolina to New York City captured students' interest, especially when the friend's wife appears to be completely different than how

---

[19] Poe, Edgar Allan. "The Oblong Box." The Works of Edgar Allan Poe – Volume 4, The Raven Edition. Project Gutenberg, 10 Nov. 2012, gutenberg.org/files/2150/2150-h/2150-h.htm#link2H_4_0013.

she had been described in their correspondence. We discussed possible themes of the work, and students were quick to see how a person could go crazy if he or she could not grieve openly.

"What literary devices does Poe use to convey his theme?" I asked the class.

Thomas was quick to answer, "Well, point of view is kind of important."

"That's good. Tell everyone why," I prodded him.

"The narrator is finding out what's going on and what's in the box, and we're finding out at the same time," he added. "You know there's something going on, but you don't find out until the end."

"I'd call that suspense, wouldn't you?" I said. "So the first person point of view adds to the suspense since we find out what's in the box at the same time the narrator does. What other literary devices do you see at work?" I saw Charlie's hand beginning to pump the air. "Hannah, what do you see?"

Hannah stopped talking to the girl beside her for a moment and then said, "I don't know," as if she thought that would give her a free pass not to think about the essay.

"OK," I told her. "Where does this story take place?"

"On a boat," she said with a roll of the eyes as if I were a little stupid to be asking that question.

"If this story had taken place on land, would there have been a story? Would the artist need to keep it a secret that his beloved wife was dead in the box? Would the narrator be able to hear him cry as he pried open the box each night if they weren't on a small ship?" I pressed her.

"No," she said. "It had to take place on a boat for the story to work."

"What literary element is that? The story taking place on a boat?"

"Setting?" she questioned as if there might be another possibility.

"Yes! Good job!" I praised her though I had done much of the heavy lifting in thinking that one through. "Charlie, what literary element do you see?"

"Diction!" he said in a loud voice. "I like where the narrator says, 'The salt! I ejaculated.'" Charlie grinned and looked around at the other students, pleased with his innuendo.

The other students looked disgusted with his junior high joke, and though I knew he was trying to get a laugh, it failed miserably. "I think there are other examples of diction in there. Who has one ready?" The discussion continued onward, but Charlie looked disappointed that no one laughed. It was the first of many times that he tried to connect with his classmates, but his eccentricities and immaturity got in the way.

Another day in class we were discussing Temple Grandin's essay "Thinking in Pictures." She shared how it felt to be autistic, how she learned, and how she was often misunderstood.[20] "So how do autistic people learn?" I asked the class. Out of the corner of my eye, I noticed Charlie's hand up in the air, but I intentionally called on someone at the back of the room. "Miranda, do you remember from Grandin's essay how they learn best?"

"I think it said something about needing pictures or images for something to make sense to them," Miranda said as she flipped through the pages, pushing her cell phone under a notebook.

"Good," I praised her effort, knowing how difficult it can be to remember the main point of an essay when you're reading the latest tweets. "How did she learn abstract words, like peace, or prepositions like under?"

Todd's hand ventured up, but Charlie's was urgently pumping up and down. "Todd, how did she learn words like peace or under?"

"She would like picture in her head getting under a desk or something," Todd struggled, but then it came to him. "Oh, yeah. And she thought of peace like a dove."

"That's right. She also encountered trouble at school with her peers. Who remembers that story?"

Charlie was practically standing up at this point, sitting on one knee, right arm stretched high in the air. "Charlie, what happened with Grandin's peers at school?"

---

[20] Grandin, Temple. "Thinking in Pictures." *The Millennium Reader*, Pearson, Inc., 2009, pp. 231-235.

Charlie put his arm down, probably to restore the circulation, and said, "The kids at school called her 'tape recorder' because she would always repeat what they said, and they called her 'bones' because she was so skinny."

"How did she respond to that treatment? Did she understand what was happening?" I asked him.

Charlie moved off his knee and sat in his chair. He paused for a moment which was unlike him. "She felt like a social dud, she says in the book, and she didn't understand why they were mean to her," he said softly.

I thought he was going to go on, but he didn't. He seemed to be out of words, a rarity for him, so I moved on to the next question about the text and called on another student. Charlie was attentive for the rest of the class but not his usual commanding, boisterous self. I wondered if the term "social dud" made him relate to Grandin. If it did, I hoped that Grandin's successes would give him the encouragement and hope that life would be OK despite his ADHD and Tourette syndrome.

Coming to class one day, I saw Charlie sitting outside, and when he spotted me, he raised his hand in a high-five gesture. Though I couldn't remember ever high-fiving a student before, I lightly slapped his palm and said, "How's it going, Charlie?"

"I'm running into some trouble with this research, Mrs. Kuhlman," he said as he followed me into the classroom. "I've found sources that suggest obesity could be reduced if people didn't use microwave ovens, but I'm not sure it's enough to write six pages."

In the few minutes before class started, I quickly did a search, and I suggested that he consider the practical aspect: people would be less likely to heat up processed, unhealthy boxed meals without a microwave. It was a stretch, but together we found a few credible websites that provided some information, and we worked to change his thesis statement to accommodate this.

Rough drafts of their largest writing project were collected a few weeks later, and my job was to go through them, offering feedback to prevent them from bombing the final essay, their most important assignment. After staying up going through research papers until well after midnight, my usual patient demeanor was as thin and fragile as a piece of antique parchment. I wearily made my way into the classroom, unpacked my materials for the day, and began the class. Before I could even finish outlining what was to be covered that day, Charlie had interrupted me, "Mrs. Kuhlman!" with his hand thrusting into the air with urgency.

"What?" I snapped. Charlie put his hand down, and the class looked around at each other uncomfortably. Charlie spoke softly, "I just wanted to tell you I looked at those websites you helped me find, and they were really helpful with my problem-solving essay."

Instantly I was remorseful and apologetic. "I'm sorry, Charlie, for sounding impatient. I've had a few late nights lately." My excuse sounded lame and self-serving. "I'm glad that you found the websites helpful. Thanks for sharing." I continued the class, but I was mindful of the way the students avoided asking questions, fearful of another terse response.

I continued to go through the rough drafts of the advanced composition classes. Between the four classes, I had over one hundred students, plus homeschooling two of my own children. This created more late nights; 1:00 am became my normal bedtime, rising again at 6:00 am to start all over again. Weekends were more grading and fielding student emails. Because the end of the semester was only a couple of weeks away, I only had a short time to complete my rough draft review. Once I made it through them all, I announced it in each class.

After I made the announcement that the rough draft reviews were completed, Charlie came up to me. "Mrs. Kuhlman, I didn't get my rough draft review back yet," he said timidly, almost as if he were hurt by my oversight.

Mortified, I looked through the student files on my flash drive and in my email. All the other ninety-nine drafts were done, but Charlie's draft wasn't. "I'm so sorry, Charlie. I'll do it as soon as I get home, and you'll have it by this evening," I said, feeling terrible that I had overlooked his essay. "I'll give you five points extra credit for my error," attempting to make right more wrongs than just this one.

I went home that day and reviewed Charlie's essay. Although I initially doubted his argument about microwaves and their potential link to obesity, he wrote about the topic in a compelling way, utilizing sources and creating connections that I hadn't considered. After I emailed my feedback to him as promised, I began to work on dinner. Instead of microwaving the peas that would accompany the mashed potatoes and deli rotisserie chicken that night, I decided I would cook them the old-fashioned way: on the stovetop. Charlie's argument had made me think.

After dinner, I petted my dogs, and I hugged my children (whether they wanted it or not) and my husband (who did want a hug). I told them I was so sorry for being such a grump, and they all concurred that it was true, but that they loved me anyway. I went to bed that night at 8:00 pm, knowing for sure that my teaching relies on much more than just my knowledge of sentence structure and syntax.

Just Breathe

Shelley seemed so upbeat when I met her in the Writing Lab, an open lab where any student could come for help with writing projects. She had started writing an evaluation essay, but her topic choice stumped me. Shelley wanted to review a career in law enforcement, its good points and bad, not because she was interested in a career in law enforcement but because her fiancé was interested in going into law enforcement. Her approach seemed strange as she was determined to research and interview police officers, asking their thoughts about their career's effect on family and finances. Most of her information from police officers interviewed revealed a number of hardships involved in this career. "But shouldn't this be done by your fiancé? It's really his choice, isn't it?" I asked her as she laid out all the information she had gathered.

"Well, if we're married, then his career choice will affect me and our future children, so I think he needs to know all the backstory before he commits to anything," she said matter-of-factly, smoothing her auburn hair behind her ear.

We worked to organize her information, and in the course of our conversation, Shelley shared that the previous semester had not gone well for her. "I just had so much trouble following through on assignments, so I ended up not passing my courses. This semester I have learned a lot about myself and how to study from the Success Seminar course. I want to pursue a career in naturopathic medicine, so I have a lot of schooling to go through," her green eyes sparkling with hope and promise.

I knew that the Success Seminar was a one-credit course that students who were on academic probation had to take to maintain their eligibility for financial aid. "Well, good luck with the rest of your semester, Shelley," I told her as she left the Writing Lab.

The next time I saw Shelley was shortly before the start of fall semester. I was on campus making copies, and I ran into her outside the bookstore. "Hey, Mrs. Kuhlman, do you remember me?"

"Yes, you were in the Writing Lab during the spring term, but I can't remember your name."

"It's Shelley. Guess what? I registered for your advanced composition class this fall."

"You did? Great! I guess I'll see you next week."

"You bet!"

Shelley was in the front row of my class that first day, and that became her "spot." For the first few weeks, I could count on her being in her seat before class started. One day we were discussing the Dalai Lama's essay, "The Role of Religion in Modern Society," elaborating on his point that religion can be compared to "medicine for the human spirit."[21]

One student named Darlene offered, "My daughter is diabetic, so she needs insulin, but if I take her insulin, it could hurt me. I think this example is like the point the Dalai Lama is making about certain religions working for certain people."

"That's a good example," Shelley said. "It seems to me like he is saying that religion or a person's way of relating

---

[21] Lama, Dalai. "The Role of Religion in Modern Society." *The Millennium Reader,* Pearson Education, Inc., 2009, pp. 755-761.

to God is based on how they are wired, so we can't judge others for their choices of religion. We also can't judge other religions, calling them 'weird,' because they are meeting the needs of those people or cultures that choose them." Shelley was always prepared, and she always added a quiet maturity to our class discussions.

But then she began coming in late, first five minutes, then ten, then fifteen. I assumed that she had to navigate wintery rural roads in her trek to reach campus, so I didn't think anything was wrong. When Shelley missed a few minor assignments, she came to see me in my office.

"Mrs. Kuhlman, I feel bad that I've missed these assignments, and I wanted to let you know what's going on." She had lost the sparkle that she had the first time I met her in the Writing Lab, and she seemed older, more tired, though she was only about nineteen-years-old. "I've been having panic attacks regularly. At first, I thought I was having a heart attack, but after I was checked out, nothing was wrong physically. I'm OK as long as I stay home most of the time. Today I had an attack on the way here, and I had to call my fiancé to talk me through it." Her green eyes filled with tears. "I wanted to let you know that I'm in the process of changing my diet drastically since I met with a naturopath. She's even got me taking some natural supplements and stress management techniques to help." Shelley pulled out a small, yellow tin of Bach Flower Rescue Remedy lozenges.

"Can I show you something?" I asked her, and she nodded assent. I opened my purse and pulled out a matching tin of Bach lozenges. We laughed together. "It's OK, Shelley. You can do this."

By mid-term, we were working on our largest assignment, the problem-solving essay. Shelley had chosen the topic of Generalized Anxiety Disorder (GAD), with the proposed solution of incorporating diet, exercise, and stress management techniques like meditation into a treatment plan. "Mrs. Kuhlman," she said to me one day, "did you know that forty-six percent of Americans suffer from mental health issues? Most don't seek treatment, though." The topic seemed to interest her, and she had a wealth of good sources to draw upon.

However, Shelley began missing classes. Again, I thought it was due to weather, but then she missed three weeks in a row, including the deadline for our largest writing assignment. I emailed her, but she never responded.

While I was teaching my beginning composition course the next week, I noticed Shelley standing outside the classroom's glass window. Once my class was over, I joined her in the hallway. "Hi, Shelley. How are you? What's going on?"

She started to apologize, but then the tears streamed down her cheeks. We stood there in silence for a moment, and I was unsure what to do to help. "Would you like to go into this empty classroom to talk?"

Shelley waved her hand, dismissing my suggestion, and started to take deep breaths. In through the nose and out through the mouth, in through the nose and out through the mouth. The rhythmic breathing seemed to work its magic on her, as she was finally able to speak and the tears subsided. "I know I don't deserve any accommodation, but I am asking if there is any way I could submit this essay late subject to a penalty? I am almost done with it, and I am worried about losing my financial aid if I don't pass my classes."

"Of course. Could you email it to me by tomorrow?"

"Yes, I can do that. I really, really appreciate you understanding my situation."

Her final draft of the problem-solving paper arrived the next day via email as promised, but that was the last time I saw Shelley. There were only three weeks left in the semester, and she never came back to class, missing a number of minor writing assignments and peer reviews. Her final paper, a short literary analysis, arrived by email, too, so I responded by email:

Hi Shelley,

Thanks for the final draft of the literary analysis paper. We missed you in class. You always offered thoughtful responses that were insightful and mature. However, I don't want you to beat yourself up over your grade this term. I believe that you did the best you could, given your circumstances. That said, I wanted to affirm that you are an "A" writer, even though you will most likely earn a C in my class. Your writing skills are well-developed, and you quickly learn how to improve from feedback. This will take you far when you resume your college experience, whenever that is.

Shortly after the semester ended, I received an email response from Shelley:

Hi Mrs. Kuhlman,

Thanks for your email. You're probably busy, and I really appreciate your encouraging note. I'm going to counseling now, and I'm seeing a family doctor to see if there are any health concerns I should take care of. Also, I'm glad you recommended that I research anxiety for my paper. It helped me see that I needed counseling. No matter what, I'll be okay.

Sometimes I think about Shelley as I sit quietly for twenty minutes or so in the early morning hours, spine straight, hands on my lap, breathing in and out, in and out. I listen to the high-pitched hum of silence, and I know I'm okay, too.

NAN KUHLMAN

When Learning and Life Are Hard

Phillip had no social filter. That was plain from the first day of class when he told everyone that he had flunked beginning composition the first time he took it. He also told the class, not the first day but the second day of class, that his father constantly called him stupid and occasionally beat him. Phillip's name was on my list of students who had developmental disabilities and might need special accommodations, such as extra time on quizzes or one-on-one tutoring. Phillip needed them all.

Despite his learning disability, Phillip exhibited an authenticity and a naïve, childish outlook that was refreshing. He was studying to be an RN, but he had his STNA certificate already. This enabled him to work as a caregiver for elderly or disabled people who could still live on their own. Phillip's narrative told the story of his first day at work caring for an elderly gentleman:

> I had fixed him dinner, and he was eating when he began to cough. This was nothing new, but unlike other times, this time he didn't stop coughing. He was grabbing his throat, and his face looked a little blue. I remembered the Heimlich maneuver in my STNA training, so I bent him over my arms and thrust upward at his sternum. After a couple of times, a chunk of food hit the floor. He was so grateful, and even though I was really scared, I did

a good job. That's when I knew I wanted to be a nurse because I liked how it felt to help people.

Phillip's kindness and compassion for those who were hurting were palpable, so I knew that he would make an excellent caregiver or nurse. But I wondered about his ability to make it through the difficult anatomy courses that were required for nursing. Many of my students without any learning disabilities ended up retaking these science courses as they failed to pass them the first time due to the extensive memorization that was required. Could Phillip really do the work?

Phillip's naiveté was often evident in his interactions with other students. Once he had learned a concept, such as how to properly cite a source, he would attempt to teach others as part of his peer review. The conversations would go something like this: "You see, if you want to copy something word-for-word, you have to put quotation marks around it, and then put the author's name and page number in parentheses at the end. After that, the period goes outside the parentheses, see?" The other student would look at him like he was a moron, though everything Phillip was saying was exactly correct. Phillip was oblivious to this; in his mind, he was being helpful. It was his goodhearted intentions that I found appealing.

Halloween was approaching, and our local community always hosted a Halloween parade. Anyone in a costume could walk in the parade, and spectators ended up receiving copious amounts of free candy. If one could bear the sometimes freezing temperatures of a late October evening, it was worth going to. I knew Phillip had a three-year-old daughter and three step-sons with his wife Melody, so I asked if they were going to the parade.

"No," his face clouded over with disappointment. "I have to work that evening." Phillip's face was an open book; every emotion he felt was revealed in his face.

"Well, maybe your wife could take your daughter and step-sons to the parade?" I assumed at first that he was disappointed that his kids couldn't go to the parade.

"Yeah, she might take them. But I can't go because I have to work," he said again, and I could see that his disappointment was from not being able to attend himself.

Phillip required a tutor to help with his writing projects. He was always disciplined about meeting with her, and he was very good about juggling his school workload with his work schedule. Between the help I provided and the tutor, Phillip did very well in class, but I wondered if he would be able to apply what he learned in our class to his next classes when it came to writing papers. Retention seemed to be a problem for him.

The next semester in the spring Phillip showed up at my office. He was in advanced composition with an instructor who had been called "unhelpful" by some students. Phillip had met with the instructor to ask for help in figuring out a theme for a literary analysis of a work, but true to his reputation, the instructor told Phillip that his suggested theme was incorrect, yet he would not offer a better alternative.

I didn't have time to help Phillip right then as I was headed to a class, but I suggested that he get a tutor, just like he had with my class. "I did get a tutor, but she doesn't know how to figure out the theme, either," he said with a long face. "If I don't figure this out, I'm going to fail this class. I don't know what I'm going to do."

My heart went out to him, but I did not have the time to make his problem my problem. "Try the Writing Lab," I offered. "The tutors in there are faculty members, so they might be able to help."

He picked up his backpack, thanked me, and trudged toward the lab. He was disappointed that I couldn't help, yet I knew that I couldn't take him on and carry my course load. He needed to figure out if college was for him before he took on too many grants that would have to be repaid if he dropped out.

Phillip's wife Melody registered for my beginning composition course the next fall term. She was lovely, but it was clear that she was the dominant partner in the relationship. When Phillip was doing group work in a sociology class and one of their group members was slacking, it wasn't Phillip who confronted him; it was Melody. She was a force to be reckoned with, and she freely admitted that she suffered from bipolar disorder and was taking medication for it.

She stayed after class one day, and I sensed she wanted to talk to me. Melody had not been her usual talkative self that day in our class discussion, so I thought something was up. "What's the matter, Melody? You don't seem like yourself today," I said.

"The doctor changed my medication, and now I can't sleep. I haven't slept for a couple days," she said, putting her face in her hands. "On top of that my mom is getting out of prison, and she needs a place to stay. She's been locked up for drug dealing for a couple of years. I'm not sure I want her to stay with us, but I'm trying to forgive her so I feel like I should." Melody went on to explain that her mother was a drug addict, often leaving a six-year-old Melody unsupervised and in charge of her two younger sisters for days at a time. She told about learning to cook macaroni and cheese by looking at the pictures because she couldn't read the recipe instructions. Her mother brought home boyfriends who ended up sexually abusing Melody and her sisters. Later, because of undiagnosed bipolar disorder and depression, Melody's first husband had her committed to a mental hospital so that he could divorce her more easily and marry his mistress. The words poured out of her like water from a fire hose. I was left reeling and uncertain what to say, so I listened and put my hand on her arm.

"Do you need to talk to a counselor? We have counseling services available for free," I offered as I noticed Phillip coming into the classroom looking for her.

"No, it's OK. Phillip and I go to a really great church, and we talk to our pastor about the whole situation. He helps us make sense of it all," she said as she wiped her eyes with a tissue.

Phillip came up and put a hand on her shoulder. "Are you OK, Mel? Let's go home and see if you can get some sleep," he said, gently helping her to her feet and picking up her backpack. The two of them walked out of the classroom as I watched them, still shaking my head over the resilience of the human spirit.

By the end of the term, Melody had reached her stride. She was an excellent writer, and she quickly grasped the nuances of documenting sources. "Hey, Mrs. Kuhlman, guess what?" she said after class one day. "I'm transferring to Butler University, and it looks like I'll get a full ride."

"Good for you, Melody! You deserve it. You're a very good writer, and you've proven that you can really form a good argumentative essay," I praised her.

"I got some bad news, though. Phillip is going to drop out. He says he can't take all the schoolwork; it's just too hard for him."

I had suspected that might be the case, but I had hoped that Phillip might be able to rise to the challenge. "I'm so sorry to hear that. Will you have to pay back loans or grants?"

"Yeah. That's what I told him, but he says he can't do it anymore. I've got to get through school and then I'll be able to help support our family," she said as she stood up to leave.

"You can do this, Melody," I assured her.

"Thanks," she said. "Your encouragement has meant a lot. My mom is coming out to campus today. She's been living with us and helping look after the kids while I work at Sears and go to school. I'd like her to meet you."

"Sure," I said with more positivity than I felt. I remembered Melody's stories of her mother leaving her children for days on end, exposing her daughters to sexual predators and then disbelieving them when they told her about it. I wasn't sure I wanted to meet this woman, but since Melody had been working on forgiving her mother, it was clear that I should, too.

"Here she is! Mom, come in here and meet Mrs. Kuhlman," Melody called out in the hallway. A woman about my age with bleached blonde hair came into the classroom. "Mom, this is Mrs. Kuhlman, my English teacher."

I stuck out my hand. "It's nice to meet you. Melody has done a fabulous job this semester. She's quite a writer."

Melody's mother took my hand and shook it limply. She smiled and said, "Nice to meet you, too," and at that moment, I saw fear, shame, regret, and disappointment written in the deep lines of her face. I saw the times I let my own children down when my failings as a parent hurt them. I knew all those emotions, too, though the context might have been different. We were not so dissimilar after all.

"Well, we better get going," Melody said, ushering her mother back to the door. "My job at Sears is calling my name, I'm afraid," she laughed as they left together. I laughed, too, because shame and disappointment did not win.

Disappointment Defeated

Though I enjoyed working as an adjunct while I was still homeschooling our children, I really wanted a full-time faculty position once our youngest had graduated. As it turned out, a full-time English position opened up when one of my mentors decided to retire. Mary had been legally blind for a few years due to the degenerative effects of macular degeneration, and while she would have liked to continue for a couple more years, her eyesight would not permit it. It was bittersweet to read her letter of recommendation for me when it meant I might be taking her job:

> I believe that Nan is an excellent candidate for this position. She is well-versed in the content and current teaching trends in the discipline, and she has demonstrated a willingness to teach in any

course format: online, face-to-face, hybrid. Nan is well-respected by her colleagues, and most importantly, she cares about her students and their success.

Since few full-time positions opened up at this small community college, this one was of interest to everyone, at least as far as speculating who might have the best shot at it. It was like a horse race for these spectators, and while I didn't know if bets were placed, I knew that I was a top contender, especially having the endorsement of the incumbent. During our spring break, Dean Terry Smith called me to make sure I was applying for the position, and I took that as a good sign.

The application process was opened in early March, and the dean told me that she hoped to fill the position by the end of the spring semester, around mid-May. I already had a teaching philosophy developed and my curriculum vitae updated. I had attended a state-wide developmental education conference in Columbus (as recommended by the retiring faculty member Mary) as the new position would handle the structuring of developmental English classes. I also had registered for a June conference in Baltimore, funded by grant monies for faculty development, which featured acceleration in developmental education. The last bit of preparation I needed to do was prepare a teaching demo, using PowerPoint and including a group exercise. These I developed over spring break, and when I was back on campus for classes, I ran my presentation by my friends and colleagues.

"It's awesome, Nan!" my friend Dina said after she watched my presentation. "You know that thesis statement outline you shared with me? I showed it to my son who's a dean of general education at Indiana University. He says it's great, and he'd like to use it for some of their beginning composition classes. Is that OK?"

"Sure," I told her. "Tell him to keep me in mind if this position I'm applying for doesn't work out."

"You'll get it," Jenny chimed in, her voice loud enough that students in the hall could hear. "That presentation is really good, and you've been doing this for six years. Nobody else here has that much experience, and what's more, Mary thinks you'd be the best candidate to take her job. By the way, the outline you helped me create for my humanities class has really worked well. The students seem to understand better what they're supposed to write about."

"I don't know, guys," I said, feeling a little doubtful. "It's already April, and they still haven't scheduled first interviews yet. I asked the dean, and she said they accepted another round of applications. It sounds like they didn't feel they had enough worthy applicants." I had heard of the interactions the dean had had with other adjuncts: bypassing them when it came to assigning classes, ignoring their emails, procrastinating on class assignments. Though she had never dealt with me in this manner, I was on guard.

"If you don't get it, I'll be really surprised," Dina said as the two of them started out the office door for class. "Keep us posted!"

April turned into May, and May morphed into June. The dean said coordinating the schedules of the six-member search committee was the reason for the delay. I was scheduled to fly to Baltimore, Maryland, with another full-time faculty member to attend the conference in three weeks, and I didn't know if I had the job. In fact, the reason I had agreed to go to the conference was to prepare me for this full-time position.

Finally, the call came. The first interview was scheduled during the first week of June. I put on my interviewing suit, stuck copies of my teaching philosophy, curriculum vitae, and Mary's letter of recommendation into my bag, and headed to the campus. The six members of the search committee, including the dean, the division secretary, two full-time English faculty, one full-time faculty member from another division, and a human resources person, sat around a table organized in a rectangular fashion. I was positioned at the head as if it were an interrogation room. All that was missing was a bright light hanging over my head.

"We'd like to thank you for expressing interest in this position," the dean said. "Each of us has a series of questions we'd like to ask, some questions based on teaching scenarios and how you would handle them and some just based on what you feel are best teaching practices."

The time went quickly, and within thirty minutes I had answered two or three rounds of their questions. Two days later I received a call inviting me back for a second interview and teaching demo. Everything seemed to be lining up, and the Baltimore conference was just ten days away.

The teaching demo was open to any employee who wished to attend, and all would complete a "scorecard" evaluating the candidate. Dina said she would attend all the demos and give me her view of the competition as well as offer me moral support. It was nice to have Dina's face in the room, though I knew or at least had seen everyone who was in there. With my presentation loaded up, I began, "Thank you all for being here today. This is Composition I, and today we're going to discuss how to construct an effective argumentative thesis statement, and then talk about how to use that statement to create an outline we can follow in writing our assignment."

I had practiced and practiced my presentation with my husband, and he had helped me weed out the "umm-ms" I sometimes inserted as I grappled for a word. I only noticed saying "umm-m" two times throughout the presentation, and other than that, I couldn't have done any better.

Later that day, Dina emailed me. I knew I could trust her to be upfront with me, and her intuition was keen:

You have one serious competitor, and if she beats you out, you should feel no shame whatsoever. I gave you both 20/20 on the scoresheet even though I really looked for ways I could mark her down. :) Shame on me! I know how you work so I would choose you, but others may not do that. The other candidates received 15 and 9 from me so you can see the wide spread. I would be upset if the 9 got it and pissed if the 15 did, but I don't think they will as the contrast was just too great. I wish you luck. Be proud of yourself and be glad you had this experience. It's all good. I'll keep my fingers crossed.

As I read her email, I had a flashback to my senior year in high school. The year before I had a major part in the school musical *Oklahoma!* and the director pulled me aside before the summer break. "You know, if you took voice lessons over the summer, I could really see you as the lead in *South Pacific* next fall," he said to me.

I took the bait and worked on voice lessons over the summer. The problem was that the voice lessons were teaching me how to sing better, not teaching me how to sing in the roughhousing, gutsy manner that the lead character Nellie used when belting out "Honeybun," one of the slapstick solos where "Honeybun" was a soldier dressed in Polynesian drag. At the tryouts, where my voice teacher was one of the judges, I sang the songs, but I sang them without the gutsy heart that was needed. It wasn't enough, and a younger girl, a sophomore, won the lead part of Nellie.

At seventeen, I did not handle the disappointment well. I refused to talk to the winner, though she and I had been friendly acquaintances up to this point. I blamed the director; I blamed my voice teacher. Though I ended up creating a memorable humorous character out of the one line that I had, the worst part of the disappointment was telling everyone that I didn't get the part.

Right after the list went up, when my teenage emotions were still raw, my beloved band instructor (who hadn't yet seen the list) asked me, "Well, did you get the lead? We were all pulling for you." My eyes welled up, and I shook my head no. He was taken aback, and said, "I'm so sorry to hear that. I didn't mean to upset you. I thought you were a shoe-in."

These same emotions hit me when I read Dina's email about the teaching demonstrations. I wondered if this was going to be my chance to handle disappointment graciously since my immaturity prevented me from doing so last time. I had told so many people, students included, that I was applying for this job. They all hoped I would get it, and I knew they would be asking.

Within two days, I received an email letting me know that another candidate was hired. And in two more days, I was on a flight to a conference in Baltimore to help me with a job I didn't get. Weeks before, I had offered to pick up Valerie, who was full-time English faculty and part of the search committee who had hired the other candidate. By this point, I didn't even want to go, but I was committed. I decided I wasn't even going to bring up the interview; it was over and done.

As we were driving to the airport, Valerie brought up the situation: "If it's any consolation, if this candidate had interviewed when I interviewed three years ago, I wouldn't have gotten the job either. She has fifteen years teaching experience and a Ph.D. I only have an MFA."

"That makes me feel a little better," I told her. "Time and a big bag of peanut butter M&Ms will heal all wounds." She laughingly agreed, telling me that her consolation of choice was red licorice wheels or gummy bears. We talked a little more about teaching jobs, and she asked if I was going to keep looking. "Yes," I said, knowing that while my loyalty initially was to this little community college where I started, that tie had been severed when the other candidate was hired.

In the fall semester, some former students asked me if I got the full-time job. "No," I told them. "I was really disappointed at the time, but I'm OK with it. Thanks for asking." This time, admitting disappointment and defeat wasn't so bad. I sensed that change was coming, and I felt as if I were being lifted on a large wave and carried to my next assignment.

Chapter 7
Change Can Be Good

Déjà Vu

My husband, a career banker in wealth management, found himself at odds with the new emphasis in banking to grow assets and the bottom line be damned. His approach to managing a department was maintaining efficiencies to create a profit, serving customers, and working on new business leads. However, because of changes in tax law, personal trusts were no longer in favor, and given the rural demographic of the area, most people did not have sufficient assets to need a fiduciary to help manage their net worth. Though his department continually made a profit, the assets under management stayed relatively steady, and this fantasized asset growth goal became a bar that could never be reached. Craig was tired, tired of explaining why rural northwestern Ohio had few trust customers and why those few were usually content to stay with their current fiduciary. He was tired of corporate politics and in-fighting, but because of the income, he was reluctant to let the job go.

My husband and I finally decided to break the hold his banking income had on us. We reduced expenses and paid off debt, living more frugally than we had in the past. "It's like when we were first married," he joked, "and we had to pay off all our debts and save $10,000 to move out to Pasadena to go to school." He was right, but I had no clue how much like déjà vu this was.

Craig had finished his courses at Grace Communion Seminary, a seminary connected with our church. He had been taking one course per term to earn a master's in Pastoral Studies for the last eight years. Though he had considered quitting many times, he stuck with it. When he made it through the last class, he sent an email to a pastor friend named Jim who had oversight for churches in Indiana and Ohio, telling him about his achievement and reminding him of his ongoing interest in full-time ministry. This was on the heels of having five different people tell him that he should be a pastor in casual comments during the previous week.

Jim's emailed response was quick. "I talked with the head of church administration, and I'd like to come to talk in person about an idea we have." Jim lived about an hour and a half away, so Craig made plans for him to stay overnight in our spare room.

Since Jim was the regional director for pastors in Indiana and Ohio, we assumed that he had something opening up in his district. Craig had crunched the numbers and with our finances shored up and his fifty-fifth birthday in a month and a half (removing the tax penalty for accessing retirement funds), he figured that we could make it on a pastoral salary. Jim arrived and after catching up with him about his wife and kids, he moved on to the point of the trip.

"I talked with Harry, the head of church administration, and when I told him you were interested in full-time ministry, he said, 'Are you thinking what I'm thinking?' And I said, 'New Hope, right?'" Jim went on to explain that New Hope was one of the larger churches in the denomination, having over eighty-five active members, and it was located in Pasadena, California. In fact, we found out that when we lived in Pasadena twenty-five years before, we attended with the congregation that later was renamed New Hope.

A lump formed in my throat as Jim and Craig talked about details. *California? Again?* Though our children were all over the age of eighteen, how could I leave them to move across the country? How could I leave my parents, now in their eighties? I was resisting the change, though I knew it was exactly what my husband wanted and needed. I could feel myself resisting, and the tighter I held myself, the more the idea of moving across the country hurt. I knew, however, that I was going to go. The Buddhist slogan came to my mind: "Whatever you meet is the path."²² I felt myself riding a wave of change, and this point had to be the crest of the wave.

"So what do you think about this, Nan? You haven't said much," Jim asked.

"I don't know what I think. I was hoping that you had something in Indiana or Ohio, and I never dreamed that I would be moving back to Southern California," I told him. Then I looked at my husband, and I saw those golden handcuffs and all that he had put up with over the years, sucking the very joy of life from him. I remembered how I felt when I worked in insurance, and I knew that my husband had tolerated the boa constrictor around his throat long enough. "Well, I didn't really want to go the last time we moved out there, but I'll have to say it was one of the best decisions we ever made," I said. "So I guess I'll trust that this will also be a good decision. Just be patient with me. I mean, the last time it took ten months for me to get used to the idea, so I need some time, OK?"

Jim laughed and agreed. We went out to dinner that night, but my head was whirling with thoughts about moving and what that would mean for our grown children who still lived with us. Craig was struggling to accept that they were offering a senior pastor position to someone who, while having served in a preaching capacity locally on occasion with a brief one-year stint as a bi-vocational pastor, had never been a full-time pastor before. Jim

22 Fischer, Norman. "Life is Tough. Here are Six Ways to Deal with It." *Lion's Roar*, 7 Oct. 2016, lionsroar.com/life-is-tough-six-ways-to-deal-with-it-march-2013.

assured him that his experience in business and management had not been wasted. At the conclusion of Jim's meeting with Craig, it was agreed that we would fly out in three weeks or so during mid-September to interview with the church's advisory board, and if it went well, Craig would put in his sixty-day notice after the end of the year to capture incentive monies and stock options that were due him. We would move at the beginning of March next year.

The four-day trip to Southern California in September was a whirlwind of meetings. Though I had considerable experience in social situations because of meetings with my husband's clients over the years, I felt jet-lagged and overwhelmed. I had been asked over and over, "Aren't you concerned about leaving your eighteen-year-old behind in Ohio?" and up to that point, I had always answered that our children got along well with each other and that I was sure they would be fine.

We were in a meeting with about twenty people when I was asked again, "How do you feel about leaving your grown children?"

To my surprise, the tears began to flow uncontrollably down my face, even though I usually didn't cry easily. Crazy thoughts grabbed me: *Get it together, Nan. You're going to ruin it for him. They're going to think you don't support this.* "I know they'll be fine, but I'm still trying to get used to the idea," I said, trying to regain control. As I groped around in my purse for a tissue, I looked up to see a number of the women crying, too.

"We understand how you're feeling," one woman said who worked for the denomination's main office. "With the church headquarters moving in 2018 across the country to North Carolina, we'll be leaving our adult children here in California. We know how hard it is to come to terms with that."

I dabbed my eyes and smiled a shaky smile. Riding this wave made me feel uncertain, but it helped to know that I wasn't alone. We left California with plans to move back at the beginning of March.

School, Interrupted

The first time I saw Wayne in class, I thought he could easily be a WWE wrestler. Colorful sleeves of tattoos, a bald head, and a muscular build were his calling cards, so it made sense when I found out that he was a laid-off tire builder from a local tire manufacturer that specialized in building off-highway tires for industrial and agricultural vehicles. From what I had heard, these tires could run over six feet in diameter, so I was sure that body strength was an important asset to the job. I asked him one day after class if physical strength was important to work at the tire factory.

"Oh, hell yeah," he said. "I've probably lost fifteen pounds in muscle mass since I was laid off about six months ago. After working a shift, I'd go home, and I couldn't even hold a Gatorade bottle. It would just slip through my grasp."

"That doesn't sound like it's good for your hands and arms long-term," I said.

"Naw," Wayne continued. "When I'd sleep my arms would go numb, or they would flop around. Nervous twitches, I guess. One old guy who just retired couldn't even open his hand up anymore." He demonstrated with his own hand, holding it like a bird claw. "The guy said it hurt too bad to stretch his hand out. That would be me in about fifteen years, I bet, if I kept working there."

"I'm glad you have the chance to go to school and learn a different trade. You are really a good writer," I told him.

It seemed as if he turned a little pink, maybe a little embarrassed that his writing had depth and substance and that those grammar lessons from long ago had stuck with him. For someone who, by his own admission, prided himself on his swearing ability, it probably seemed contradictory to think that he was capable of intellectual conversation, let alone academic writing.

"Truth is, Mrs. Kuhlman," he said, "I was scared shitless to go back to school. I haven't been in school for twenty years, but this Ohio Means Jobs program came up, and because I'm laid off, they pay for my schooling and books, plus they give me unemployment to live on while I'm going to school. I mean, money's tight right now since we bought a house right before I got laid off, but if I can just get this education out of the way," his voice trailed off.

"You can do it, Wayne, and I'll bet you will be glad you did," I told him as I organized my papers for the next class. "My dad, back in the 1950s, worked at a tire factory. His dad and all his brothers worked there, and he has told me stories of how his forearms were burned from accidentally touching the hot mold. He said that at the end of a shift, the burned skin would be dangling from them. In the summer, the temperature in the plant was over one hundred degrees, and my dad said he just couldn't seem to drink enough water to make up for all that he lost through sweating."

Wayne looked at his hands, callused and scarred. "Yeah, this is the best my hands have looked in years. I was always burning them on the mold. They would scab up and then crack and bleed. Seemed like they always hurt."

"When my dad had the opportunity to apply for a job at Ohio Bell Telephone Company, he took it, even though his dad and brothers said he was crazy to take a cut in pay. He made that up over time, through stock incentives and other benefits, and he still has pretty good health now even though he's in his eighties," I said, stuffing the last of my books and papers into my rolling case to move on to the next classroom.

"That's what I'm trying to do with this schooling. I mean, we're a little pinched now, but if I can finish, it will be better in the long run," Wayne said as he picked up his backpack. We walked out into the hallway and parted ways, Wayne heading to another building for his next class and me navigating the stairs for mine.

Later I thought about our conversation, especially about the wage that the tire factory paid its workers. Wayne told me that he would clear over $1000 a week, after taxes and other deductions, though he often worked over fifty hours per week. It was easy to spend the money, he said, so he kept going back to bring it home. I could relate on a personal level with his "golden handcuffs" because of my husband's situation, and though Craig's circumstances were different than Wayne's, I could see the parallels.

One day in the hallway I saw Wayne talking to Josh, one of his buddies who also was a laid-off tire worker. They were in a huddle with a couple of other men, and I overheard them talking about getting called back to work. When Wayne saw me coming, he called me over, "Mrs. Kuhlman, some of the guys here have been called back to work. They call us back based on when we started. Joe here started a few months before me, and he just got the call that they want him to come back and work third shift. There's one other guy with a month's more seniority than me that they'll call before they call me, so I don't know if or when I'll get a call."

He paused as he thought through the details. "I want to finish school, or I at least want to finish this semester, that way I can come back to school when they do layoffs again in January. So I'm not going to answer my phone, and if they can't reach me by phone, then they have to send me a certified letter. After that, I have two weeks to respond, so I figure that should buy me three weeks, and that will put us into November. I would only have to go to school for a month or so while working third shift, but I was wondering if you have a later class I could go to so I could have enough time to sleep?"

Wayne was in a 1:00 pm class, but that term, I also had a 4:15 pm class. "Would 4:15 pm work? I have a class then," I told him.

"Oh, yeah," he said nodding. "That would work. It would only be for a month. I probably could do it for a month," he said. His tone sounded less confident than his words, and I was disappointed that companies could disrupt these students' schedules and lives so abruptly after they were the ones who told the workers they weren't needed.

Another week or two passed, and I noticed that Wayne wasn't in class. I stopped his friend Josh on his way out the door. "Where's Wayne?"

"He went back to work," Josh said, shaking his head. "They wanted him back on first shift, and with his new house payment and everything, he couldn't turn it down, and he couldn't make school work with that schedule. So he quit school."

"If you see him, tell him I wish him well," I said to Josh. As I moved to my next classroom, I sent Wayne warm thoughts and wishes for his wellbeing, hoping that he would find a way to break the hold the factory had on him but knowing how hard that would be.

Food, Love, and Seasons

Summer wore denim skirts and modest blouses, a sharp contrast to the skinny jeans and form-fitting t-shirts worn by the majority of my female students. As I was passing back papers one day, I saw that she had a small, light brown lace doily fastened to the back of her head, though it was barely noticeable. In rural northwest Ohio, this was a tradition of those from the apostolic faith who believed that women should wear some head covering as a sign of submission to God.

Summer was part of an accelerated developmental program that put a cluster of students who needed extra writing practice in a typical beginning composition class, but also gave them a writing workshop where they could hone their skills. She was quiet, and she sat toward the back of the room.

Summer's love of cooking led her to write about the problem of childhood obesity in her rural Ohio county, offering the solution of cooking classes to help parents and children understand how to create healthful meals. Her research discovered that local youth were turning to laxatives or fasting to lose weight, and nearly half had eaten no vegetables in the week before the survey.[23]

Summer's eyes conveyed her concern when she approached me after class. "Mrs. Kuhlman, did you know that most obese children remain obese as adults? If this problem isn't addressed when these kids are in school, it could impact the nation's healthcare system."

"OK," I replied, "but how are you going to pay for these educational classes through the school? Most rural schools are running on a pretty tight budget already, and taxpayers aren't likely to approve a levy increase."

She shifted the heavy stack of printed research papers to her other arm, and said, "I've already thought that through. Local grocery stores and farms could help provide the food needed for the classes, and maybe the United Way could approach nutritionists at the local county hospitals in this area to take turns teaching the classes. The hardest part would be getting the parents to commit to attending the classes with their children, but maybe it could be tied to some extra credit with their science or health class."

Summer's plan had merit, but as she pointed out, the problem of parental follow-through was a difficult one. "What does your research say about the benefits of

---

[23] "2011 Paulding County Health Assessment." *Hcno.org*, Sep. 2011, section 9a9b pp. 1-2. hcno.org/pdf/counties/Paulding%20Co%20HA%20Final%20Report%20with%20Cover.pdf.

parental interaction with their children in these cooking classes?" I asked her.

"My sources say that parental modeling is critical in encouraging healthy eating," she responded as she leafed through her stack before pulling out the appropriate article to hand to me. "This article also says that children who observed teachers or parents eating a healthy food were more likely to try it and end up liking it, too."[24] She went on to describe her plan, one where restaurant chefs would come in to demonstrate how to create healthy versions of local favorites and gyms or other wellness centers would help sponsor cooking events in return for free advertising.

"Sounds like you've got all the bases covered," I told her. "You should give your polished final draft to the school board to see if they would consider it."

"You think they actually would listen to me?" Summer asked. "I've never done anything like that before. I don't know if I could talk about my plan before a group."

"Who says you have to talk to the whole school board? You could start with just one board member, maybe someone you know, or a friend of a friend," I suggested.

"I could, couldn't I?" she mused. The connection between love and food was strong for her, and it gave her vision and courage to see change as possible, even when it wasn't comfortable. Her view of change as something

[24] "Parental Influence on Eating Behavior." *PubMed Central* (PMC), 5 Sept. 2008, ncbi.nlm.nih.gov/pmc/articles/PMC2531152/.

potentially good would push her to see her life differently, more expansively.

One day after our writing workshop concluded, she asked if I could look through her narrative for our beginning composition class. We had had a peer review that day, and from what I could tell, her peer reviewer had torn her paper to shreds. I saw comments like, "Too many memories. Need to show better examples." I wondered if her essay really was that bad, so I began to read.

Her narrative started talking about change, how we often want life to remain the same when it is good and satisfying. She shared her feelings about her older sister's engagement, knowing that their relationship was closing a season they both treasured and that it would be different. Summer wrote, "I wanted my sister to be happy, to be married, if that's what she wanted. I wondered if we would still have time for each other. I knew deep down that her priorities would change. Her husband had to come first, and when children came, they would also demand her time. How would she have time for me?"

She shared her fondest memories of their sister bond. One time they were working outside after a hard rain, and Summer said that she felt a clump of dirt hit her shoulder. She looked up, and there was her sister, holding handfuls of mud, ready to pummel her with dirt clods. Summer took up the dirt clod challenge, and before they were done, they both were muddy from head to toe. Her sister's fiancé videotaped the mock fight, and Summer told of watching and re-watching that video after her sister's engagement announcement, tears flowing.

Another memory she shared was where she and her sister were baking a large number of cookies for a church fundraiser. After the batch was mixed and a number of them baked, they decided to taste their handiwork only to realize that they forgot to add the sugar. This created a standing joke between them any time either of them was going to bake cookies: "Don't forget the sugar!" The narrative was full of fond memories of a close, sisterly bond.

Her narrative told about how even beautiful relationships must change, that seasons of life begin and end, and that grieving the change is normal. It spoke volumes to me about the changes facing me personally in the next few months, ones that I was already grieving and fearful and excited about all at the same time. "It's beautiful and perfect as is," I said as I handed the rough draft back to her, blinking away tears.

Letting Go

I knew I couldn't teach any face-to-face classes, my preference and specialty, during the spring term because our California move was scheduled for the beginning of March. I wanted to keep my toe in teaching, at least teaching online, but I knew that Dean Terry Smith expected me to help with the developmental writing courses. In fact, she had sent me an email about a conference in Columbus and asked me to set up a meeting with her to discuss my role in the department's efforts to scale up the accelerated learning program. "Do I tell her or not?" I asked my husband.

"I don't know. You have to decide that," he responded, no help at all.

I set up a meeting with her at her request, planning to simply tell her that I wanted to only teach online during the spring term to finish my book, the book I started as part of my master's program. I planned to ask for two online courses, but I wasn't going to share about our long-distance move. My internal wrestling, though, made me doubt this initial decision, and even as I walked toward the dean's office, I wasn't sure what I should do.

"We are excited about scaling up our developmental program," Dean Smith told me in her office. "With only you and Valerie teaching the embedded developmental classes, we could only serve about twenty of the ninety students who qualified to be in the program." She paused to let this sink in. "I have been telling our Vice President of Academic Affairs that we need another full-time person to pull this off, and I think she's beginning to hear me. I need to know if you want to be a part of this process."

Tell her, the voice in my head said. *Tell her,* it repeated. I was gambling here, but I wanted to be as upfront and honest as I could be. I didn't want her depending on my participation when I knew I would be moving in six months. I cared deeply about the college and especially its developmental learners. *Tell her*, the voice insisted.

"Can I shut your door?" I asked her. I then told her the truth: that I would be moving in less than six months, not because I wanted to go but because my husband needed to go. I asked her to keep this confidentially between us, as my husband would not be giving notice until February. "Teaching those students means the world to me, and it is with a heavy heart that I leave," I told her, my eyes beginning to tear. "Would you be willing to let me teach online, even if I were in another state?"

"It's important that I know I have good online instructors," she said in an affirming but noncommittal way. Then she rose from her chair, came around her desk and shook my hand, thanking me for all the work I had done for her and for the college. I felt odd; I had expected her to give me a quick hug and a reassurance of her support, especially given that the full-time position I was practically promised went to someone else and since I had always done anything she had ever asked of me. I left that day hoping that she would keep her word but knowing how little influence adjuncts have. For every part-time instructor who leaves, there are always more to take her place.

I waited for the spring term classes to be assigned. I put my request in for two beginning composition classes or two advanced composition classes online. While other institutions had already assigned their classes, oftentimes two semester terms in advance, Ohio Community College, at least the Arts & Sciences division, never had the spring term schedule confirmed until at least Thanksgiving. I continued to check the schedule, looking to see if part-time instructors were being assigned. One weekend I noticed that all the classes were assigned; I was given none. There was no email explanation; my name was simply omitted from the list.

My initial response was to berate myself for telling the dean in the first place. *I should have acted like I was all in,* later realizing that she would have known something was up when I declined to teach face-to-face courses. I would have had to lie, and ultimately, it would be the students who paid, not having an instructor prepared and ready to help. Still, I couldn't just let it go. I emailed the dean:

> I am looking through the schedule for the spring term, and I don't see where I have been assigned any online Composition I or II classes as we discussed. Are there other sections available?

Her response was quick, quicker than I had ever experienced with her before:

> I'm sorry, but I didn't see your name on any adjunct faculty course requests. It slipped my mind that we had discussed it, so I didn't assign you any for that reason only. Perhaps I can meet with you

later in the week when you come to campus. My schedule has been somewhat hectic, but I'm happy to discuss this with you.

There was nothing to discuss. All available classes had been assigned. My current students had been asking when I was going to be assigned, and now I was going to have to explain somehow that I wasn't offered any, not even online. It was déjà vu all over again, just as I had to explain why I didn't get the full-time job, only this time, I couldn't reveal the reason for not teaching face-to-face. My husband needed to collect his year-end bonus and stock options (not available until February) if we were going to make it on retirement savings and a pastor's salary.

"I guess there are only just so many sections available," I told one student. "The dean decides who gets the few sections available for part-time instructors. You could talk to her if there aren't any sections that work for you. Maybe she'll open more sections."

"I was hoping you'd be teaching face-to-face next term," he said as he looked down at a worn camo backpack in his hands, unsure of himself and his newfound writing ability.

"I know," I told him. "You'll be fine," I said, trying to reassure us both.

During the week of Thanksgiving break, I was going through rough drafts for my beginning composition classes' final project. As I flipped through my active class assignments in search of a student email address, I saw it: one online advanced composition class assigned to me for the spring term. Gratitude welled up, along with tears. The students at this little, rural community college were my people, and I had been struggling to let go. I already was leaving my own grown children, and the thought of leaving my Ohio students added another layer to my shadow of grief. This online class would help me transition, keeping something familiar and known close to my heart while moving so far from home.

Epilogue

The first day of classes in August was unusually warm, and high temperatures in the eighties with lots of sun and humidity made it seem more like summer term than fall term. Though typically I taught in the mornings, this fall term my schedule ran in the afternoon, from around 1:00 pm to 7:00 pm. I had just started going over the syllabus in my last class, a developmental writing workshop, when a student in the back said, "Excuse me, but I just received a text alert on my phone that says there's a tornado warning for Defiance County."

Defiance County was a neighboring county, so I checked my phone. A text message from my daughter said, "Tornado warning here. We are in the crawl space." Since we did not have a basement at our house, we would move to the crawl space under the house which was pretty nice (for a crawl space), with lights and about four feet of room to sit upright on a loose gravel floor. For my daughter to go down there without being told, that meant the weather situation must look threatening.

I was surprised that no one in security had come around to tell us, so I had all the students gather their belongings, and we went downstairs to the security office. When I asked if the officer knew details about the storm, he said, "Yes, ma'am. I'm watching the radar right now. The tornado warning has not yet hit our county, but as soon as it does..."

With that, a loud screech came through his weather alert system. The county Ohio Community College was in now had a tornado warning, too. We were told to move to the newest building in the college, and we were directed to a long hallway that was marked "Tornado Shelter." Faculty and students alike moved through the hallway, seeking space to stand, and I overheard a couple of instructors discussing how these walls were built to withstand winds of over three hundred miles per hour. *Well, I guess I'm better off here than I would be in our crawl space*, I thought, trying to make the best of the situation though I was worried about my family and my dogs at home.

I settled against the wall, near the doors where students and instructors from all the evening classes were coming in to seek shelter. I leaned against the wall and traded a Snapchat with my daughter of my high-heeled pumps, clearly the wrong shoes to wear if one has to stand in a concrete hallway for a long time. As I scanned the faces of the students entering the hallway, I saw familiar ones.

"Hi, Michael. How are you?" I said, noticing he was still wearing a black beanie.

"Doin' great, Mrs. K. And how are you?"

"A little hot in this stuffy hallway. It's good to see you here."

"You, too, Mrs. K," he said as he continued down the hall to join a group of other guys who also wore beanies of varying hues.

I saw her auburn hair and quick smile before she saw me. "Hi, Shelley. How's it going?"

She glanced at me, and her face broke into a wide smile. She hugged me, and said, "Thanks so much for the email you sent. I'm back at school this term, and I'm doing much better."

"That's great to hear, Shelley. Take care."

"You, too," Shelley said as she moved with the steady stream of students down the hallway.

I saw former student after former student walk by me as I waited out the storm with them. I was able to see how they were doing, and I was encouraged that they were still in school, especially since I knew some of the challenges they faced. Together we waited out the storm in that hot, stuffy hallway, and we knew that we would be safe. Though it would be the last term I taught face-to-face at this little community college, I took with me some of the hope and promise in that hallway. My future students in California would need that resilience and confidence, and I planned to graciously pass it along to them.

About the Author

Nan Kuhlman is an author, freelance writer, and part-time university professor who lives in Los Angeles but still thinks of rural northwest Ohio as home.

Nan currently works as a technical writer in Los Angeles, but because her freelancing career has spanned more than two decades, she can't break her streak and continues to freelance in her free time. You can read her eclectic collection of writing at nankuhlman.com.

Selected Other Titles
from Annorlunda Books

Original Short eBooks and Collections

Academaze, by Sydney Phlox, is a collection of essays and cartoons about the tenure track and beyond at a research university.

Both Sides of My Skin, by Elizabeth Trach, is a collection of short stories exploring the reality of pregnancy and motherhood.

The Burning, by J.P. Seewald, is a novella set in the coal country of Pennsylvania, about a family struggling to cope as a slow-moving catastrophe threatens everything they have..

The Inconvenient God, by Francesca Forrest, is a fantasy novelette about a government official tasked with retiring a god who isn't quite ready to leave.

The Lilies of Dawn, by Vanessa Fogg, is a fantasy novelette about love, duty, family, and one young woman's coming of age.

Water into Wine, by Joyce Chng, is a sci-fi novella about a family trying to build a life amidst an interstellar war that threatens everything.

About the Publisher

Annorlunda Books is a small press that publishes books to inform, entertain, and make you think. We publish short writing (novella length or shorter), fiction or non-fiction.

Find more information about us and our books online at annorlundaenterprises.com/books, on Facebook at @annorlundabooks, or on Twitter at @AnnorlundaInc.

To stay up to date on all of our releases, subscribe to our mailing list at:

annorlundaenterprises.com/mailing-list/

Caresaway, by DJ Cockburn, is a near future "inside your head" thriller about a scientist who discovers a cure for depression, but finds that it comes at a terrible cost.

Unspotted, by Justin Fox, is the story of the Cape Mountain Leopard, the scientist dedicated to saving these rare and elusive big cats, and the author's own journey to try to see one.

Okay, So Look and *Here's the Deal*, by Micah Edwards, are humorous, accurate and thought-provoking, retelling of The Books of Genesis and Exodus.

Don't Call It Bollywood, by Margaret E. Redlich, is an introduction to the world of Hindi film.

Taster Flights

Hemmed In is a collection of classic short stories about women's lives.

Love and Other Happy Endings is a collection of classic short love stories that all end on a high note.

Missed Chances is another Taster Flight of classic stories about love and "the one that got away."

Small and Spooky is a collection of classic ghost stories that feature a child. These stories are spooky with a hint of sweet.